Words of the Ancient Wise, From Epictetus and Marcus Aurelius

WORDS OF THE ANCIENT WISE

Un   ®

Un ⋅ ®

WORDS OF
THE ANCIENT WISE

FROM EPICTETUS AND
MARCUS AURELIUS

BY

W. H. D. ROUSE
M.A., LITT.D.

METHUEN & CO.
36 ESSEX STREET W.C.
LONDON

These extracts are taken from the translations
of *Marcus Aurelius* by MERIC CASAUBON (1634
and 1635), and of *Epictetus* by ELIZABETH
CARTER (1758) *A few corrections, alterations,
and omissions have been made.*

First Published in 1906

Un

WORDS OF
THE ANCIENT WISE

A DAY BOOK OF EPICTETUS AND MARCUS AURELIUS

JANUARY 1

IN the morning as soon as thou art awaked, when thy judgment, before either thy affections, or external objects have wrought upon it, is yet most free and impartial : put this question to thyself, whether if that which is right and just be done, the doing of it by thyself, or by others when thou art not able thyself, be a thing material or no. For sure it is not. And as for these that keep such a life, and stand so much upon the praises, or dispraises of other men, hast thou forgotten what manner of men they be : that such and such upon their beds, and such at their board : what their ordinary actions are : what they pursue after, and what they fly from · what thefts and rapines they commit, if not with their hands and feet, yet with that more precious part of theirs, their minds : which (would it but admit of them) might enjoy faith, modesty, truth, justice, a good spirit.

M. A. x. 15.

IN the morning when thou findest thyself unwilling to rise, consider with thyself presently,
it is to go about a man's work that I am stirred
up. Am I then yet unwilling to go about that,
for which I myself was born and brought forth
into this world? Or was I made for this, to lay
me down, and make much of myself in a warm
bed ?

M. A. v. 1.

WHEN thou art hard to be stirred up and
awaked out of thy sleep, admonish thyself
and call to mind, that to perform actions tending
to the common good is that which thine own
proper constitution, and that which the nature
of man doth require. But to sleep, is common
to unreasonable creatures also.

M. A. viii. 11.

NOT to be slack and negligent ; or loose, and
wanton in thy actions, nor contentious, and
troublesome in thy conversation, nor to rove
and wander in thy fancies and imaginations
Not basely to contract thy soul ; nor boisterously
to sally out with it, or, furiously to launch out
as it were, nor ever to want employment.

M. A. viii. 19.

2

BETIMES in the morning say to thyself: This day I shall have to do with an idle curious man, with an unthankful man, a railer, a crafty, false, or an envious man; an unsociable uncharitable man. All these ill qualities have happened unto them, through ignorance of that which is truly good and truly bad. But I that understand the nature of that which is good, that it only is to be desired, and of that which is bad, that it only is truly odious and shameful: who know moreover, that this transgressor, whosoever he be, is my kinsman, not by the same blood and seed, but by participation of the same reason, and of the same divine particle; How can I either be hurt by any of those, since it is not in their power to make me incur anything that is truly reproachful? or angry, and ill affected towards him, who by nature is so near unto me? for we are all born to be fellow-workers, as the feet, the hands, and the eye-lids; as the rows of the upper and under teeth: for such therefore to be in opposition, is against nature; and what is it to chafe at, and to be averse from, but to be in opposition?

M. A. i. 15.

THIS is the nature of our proceedings. As in a crowded fair the horses and cattle are brought to be sold, and the greatest part of men come either to buy or sell; but there are a few who come only to look at the fair, and inquire how it is carried on; and why in that manner; and who appointed it; and for what purpose: thus, in the fair of the world, some, like cattle, trouble themselves about nothing but fodder. For as to all you who busy yourselves about possessions and farms and domestics and public posts, these things are nothing else but mere fodder. But there are some few men among the crowd who are fond of looking on and considering, "What then, after all, is the world? Who governs it? Hath it no governor? How is it possible, when neither a city nor a house can remain ever so short a time without someone to govern and take care of it, that this vast and beautiful system should be administered in a fortuitous and disorderly manner? Is there then a governor? What sort of one is he? And how doth he govern; and what are we who are under him; And for what designed? Have we some connection and relation to him; or none?" In this manner are the few affected; and apply themselves only to view the fair and then depart.

E. D. ii. 14, 4.

IN every affair consider what precedes and follows, and then undertake it Otherwise you will begin with spirit; but not having thought of the consequences, when some of them appear you will shamefully desist. "I would conquer at the Olympic games." But consider what precedes and follows, and then, if it be for your advantage, engage in the affair. You must conform to rules, submit to a diet, refrain from dainties; exercise your body, whether you choose it or not, at a stated hour, in heat and cold; you must drink no cold water, nor sometimes even wine. In a word, you must give yourself up to your master, as to a physician. Then, in the combat, you may be thrown into a ditch, dislocate your arm, turn your ankle, swallow abundance of dust, be whipped, and, after all, lose the victory. When you have reckoned up all this, if your inclination still holds, set about the combat. Otherwise, take notice, you will behave like children, who sometimes play wrestlers, sometimes gladiators, sometimes blow a trumpet, and sometimes act a tragedy, when they happen to have seen and admired these shows. Thus you too will be at one time a wrestler, at another a gladiator, now a philosopher, then an orator; but with your whole soul, nothing at all. Like an ape, you mimic all you see, and one thing after another is sure to please you, but is out of favour as soon as it becomes familiar. For you have never entered upon anything considerately, nor after having viewed the whole matter on all sides, or made any scrutiny into it, but rashly, and with a cold inclination.

E. D. iii. 15, 1.

THE natural properties, and privileges of a reasonable soul are; That she seeth herself; that she can order, and compose herself: that she makes herself as she will herself. that she reaps her own fruits whatsoever, whereas plants, trees, unreasonable creatures, what fruit soever (be it either fruit properly, or analogically only) they bear, they bear them unto others, and not to themselves. Again; Whensoever, and wheresoever, sooner or later, her life doth end, she hath her own end nevertheless. For it is not with her, as with dancers, and players, who if they be interrupted in any part of their action, the whole action must needs be imperfect. but she in what part of time or action soever she be surprised, can make that which she hath in her hand whatsoever it be, complete and full, so that she may depart with that comfort, "I have lived; neither want I anything of that which properly did belong unto me."

M. A. xi. 1.

YOU say theorems are useless. To whom?
To such as apply them ill. For medicines
for the eyes are not useless to those who apply
them when and as they ought. Fomentations
are not useless; poisers are not useless; but they
are useless to some, and, on the contrary, useful
to others. If you should ask me now, Are
syllogisms useful? I answer, that they are useful;
and, if you please, I will show you how. "Will
they be of service to me, then?"—Why, did you
ask, man, whether they would be useful to you, or
in general? If anyone in a dysentery should ask
me whether acids be useful, I answer, They are.
"Are they useful for me, then?"—I say, No.
First try to get the flux stopped, and the exulcera-
tion healed. Do you, too, first get your ulcers
healed; your fluxes stopped. Quiet your mind,
and bring it free from distraction to the school,
and then you will know what is the force of
reasoning.

E. D. ii. 21, 3.

WHY should I grieve myself; who never did willingly grieve any other! One thing rejoiceth one, and another thing another. As for me, this is my joy; if my understanding be right and sound, as neither averse from any man, nor refusing any of those things, which as a man I am subject unto; if I can look upon all things in the world meekly and kindly; accept all things, and carry myself towards everything according to the true worth of the thing itself.

M. A. viii. 41.

WHEN one consulted him, how he might persuade his brother to forbear treating him ill: Philosophy, answered Epictetus, doth not promise to procure anything external to man, otherwise it would admit something beyond its proper subject-matter. For the subject-matter of a carpenter is wood; of a statuary, brass: and so of the art of living, the subject-matter is each person's own life.

E D. i. 15, 1

WELL then : each of the animals is constituted either for food, or husbandry, or to produce milk, and the rest of them for some other like use ; and for these purposes what need is there of understanding the appearances of things, and being able to make distinctions concerning them ? But God hath introduced man as a spectator of Himself and His works, and not only as a spectator, but an interpreter of them. It is therefore shameful that man should begin and end where irrational creatures do. He is indeed rather to begin there, but to end where nature itself hath fixed our end ; and that is in contemplation and understanding, and in a scheme of life comformable to nature.

E. D. i 6, 4.

9

Un

NO object can of itself beget any opinion in
us, neither can come to us, but stands without still and quiet; but we ourselves beget, and
as it were print in ourselves opinions concerning
them. Now it is in our power, not to print them;
and if they creep in and lurk in some corner, it
is in our power to wipe them off. Remember
moreover, that this care and circumspection of
thine, is to continue but for a while, and then thy
life will be at an end. And what should hinder,
but that thou mayst do well with all these
things? For if they be according to nature, rejoice in them, and let them be pleasing and
acceptable unto thee. But if they be against
Nature, seek thou that which is according to thine
own Nature, and whether it be for thy credit or
no, use all possible speed for the attainment of
it: for no man ought to be blamed, for seeking
his own good and happiness.

M. A. xi. 15.

WHAT was it, that waked Epicurus from his sleep, and compelled him to write what he did? What else but that which is of all others the most powerful in mankind, nature; which draws everyone, however unwilling and reluctant, to its own purposes? For since, says she, you think that there is no relation between mankind, write this doctrine, and leave it for the use of others, and break your sleep upon that account; and, by your own practice, confute your own principles. Do we say that Orestes was roused from sleep by the agitation of the Furies, and was not Epicurus waked by Furies more cruel and avenging, which would not suffer him to rest, but compelled him to divulge his own evils, as wine and madness do the priests of Cybele? So strong and unconquerable a thing is human nature! For how can a vine have the properties not of a vine, but of an olive-tree? Or an olive-tree not those of an olive-tree, but of a vine? It is impossible. It is inconceivable. Neither, therefore, is it possible for a human creature entirely to lose human affections. But even those who have undergone a mutilation cannot have their inclinations also mutilated : and so Epicurus, when he had mutilated all the offices of a man, of a master of a family, of a citizen, and of a friend, did not mutilate the inclinations of humanity . . . What a misfortune is it when anyone, after having received from nature standards and rules for the knowledge of truth, doth not strive to add to these, and make up their deficiencies; but, on the contrary, endeavours to take away and destroy whatever truth may be known even by them.

E. D. ii. 20, 3.

Un ®

THAT which is chief in every man's constitution, is, that he intend the common good. The second is, that he yield not to any lusts and motions of the flesh. For it is the part and privilege of the reasonable and intellective faculty, that she can so bound herself, as that neither the sensitive, nor the appetitive faculties, may not anywise prevail upon her. For both these are brutish. And therefore over both she challengeth mastery, and cannot anywise endure, if in her right temper, to be subject unto either.

M. A. vii. 30.

THEN hath a man attained to the estate of perfection in his life and conversation, when he so spends every day, as if it were his last day.

M. A. vii. 40

WHATSOEVER thou dost affect, whatsoever thou dost project, so do, and so project all, as one who, for aught thou knowest, may at this very present depart out of this life.

M. A. ii. 8.

AS it is impossible to assent to an evident falsehood, or to deny an evident truth, so it is impossible to abstain from an evident good.

E D. iii. 7, 1.

EVIDENT good at first sight attracts, and evil repels. Nor will the soul any more reject an evident appearance of good than they will Cæsar's coin.

E. D. iii. 3, 2.

A ND it is impracticable, as well as tedious, to undertake the very thing that Jupiter himself could not do · to convince all mankind what things are really good and evil. Is this granted you? The only thing granted you is to convince yourself, and you have not yet done that; and do you, notwithstanding, undertake to convince others? Why, who hath lived so long with you as you have with yourself? Who is so likely to have faith in you, in order to be convinced by you, as you in yourself? Who is a better wisher, or a nearer friend to you, than you to yourself? How is it, then, that you have not yet convinced yourself? Should not you now turn these things every way in your thoughts? What you were studying was this: to learn to be exempt from grief, perturbation, and meanness, and to be free. Have not you heard, then, that the only way that leads to this is to give up what doth not depend on choice to withdraw from it, and confess that it belongs to others? What kind of thing, then, is another's opinion about you?—"Independent on choice." Is it nothing, then, to you?— "Nothing." While you are still piqued and disturbed about it, then, do you think that you are convinced concerning good and evil?

E. D. iv. 6, 1.

Un ⋅ ®

DO but remember the general rules. What is mine? What not mine? What is allotted me? What is the will of God, that I should do now? What is not His will? A little while ago it was His will that you should be at leisure, should talk with yourself, write about these things, read, hear, prepare yourself. You have had sufficient time for this. At present He says to you, "Come now to the combat. Show us what you have learned, how you have wrestled." How long would you exercise by yourself? It is now the time to show whether you are of the number of those champions who merit victory, or of those who go about the world, conquered in all the games round. Why, then, are you out of humour? There is no combat without a tumult. There must be many preparatory exercises, many acclamations, many masters, many spectators.

E. M. iii. 2, 3.

Un   ·℗

IN short, then, remember this, that whatever
external to your own choice you esteem, you
destroy that choice. And not only power is
external to it, but the being out of power too;
not only business, but leisure too.—"Then, must
I live in this tumult now?"—What do you call
a tumult?—"A multitude of people."—And where
is the hardship? Suppose it is the Olympic
games. Think it a public assembly. There, too,
some bawl out one thing, some do another; some
push the rest. The baths are crowded. Yet
who of us is not pleased with these assemblies,
and doth not grieve to leave them? Do not be
hard to please, and squeamish at what happens.
"Vinegar is disagreeable (says one), for it is sour.
Honey is disagreeable (says a second), for it
disorders my constitution. I do not like veget-
ables, says a third. Thus, too (say others), I
do not like retirement; it is a desert: I do not
like a crowd; it is a tumult."—Why, if things are
so disposed that you are to live alone, or with
few, call this condition a repose, and make use
of it as you ought.

E. D iii. 2, 3

OF things that are external, happen what will to that which can suffer by external accidents. Those things that suffer let them complain themselves, if they will; as for me, as long as I conceive no such thing, as that that which is happened is evil, I have no hurt; and it is in my power not to conceive any such thing.

M. A. vii. 11.

MANY things there be, which oftentimes insensibly trouble and vex thee, as not armed against them with patience, because they go not ordinarily under the name of pains, which indeed are of the same nature as pain, as to slumber unquietly, to suffer heat, to want appetite when therefore any of these things make thee discontented, check thyself with these words : " Now hath pain given thee the foil: thy courage hath failed thee "

M. A. vii 36.

Un   '℞

IN the same manner as we exercise ourselves against sophistical questions, we should exercise ourselves likewise in relation to such appearances as every day occur, for these two offer questions to us. Such a one's son is dead. What do you think of it? Answer: it is independent on choice, it is not an evil.—Such a one is disinherited by his father. What do you think of it? It is independent on choice, it is not an evil.—Cæsar hath condemned him. This is independent on choice, it is not an evil.—He hath been afflicted by it. This is dependent on choice, it is an evil.—He hath supported it bravely. This is dependent on choice, it is a good.

E. D. iii. 8, 1.

WHY do you say nothing to me, then?
I have only this to say to you : That who-ever is ignorant what he is, and wherefore he was born, and in what kind of a world, and in what society; what things are good, and what evil; what fair, and what base : who understands neither discourse nor demonstration ; nor what is true nor what is false; nor is able to distinguish between them : such a one will neither exert his desires, nor aversions, nor pursuits, conformably to nature ; he will neither intend, nor assent, nor deny, nor suspend his judgment conformably to nature , but will wander up and down entirely deaf and blind, supposing himself to be somebody, while he is in reality nobody. Is there anything new in all this? Is not this ignorance the cause of all the errors that have happened from the very original of mankind?

E. D. ii. 24, 2.

E VERY great faculty is dangerous to a be-
ginner.   Study first how to live with a person
in sickness, that in time you may know how to
live with one in health.

E D. iii 13, 3.

I F you have an earnest desire of attaining to
philosophy, prepare yourself from the very first
to be laughed at, to be sneered by the multitude,
to hear them say, "He is returned to us a philosopher all at once," and "Whence this supercilious look?"   Now, for your part, do not have
a supercilious look indeed ; but keep steadily to
those things which appear best to you as one
appointed by God to this station.   For remember
that, if you adhere to the same point, those very
persons who at first ridiculed will afterwards
admire you.   But if you are conquered by them,
you will incur a double ridicule.

E. M. 22.

THE school of a philosopher is a surgery. You are not to go out of it with pleasure, but with pain : for you come there not in health ; but one of you had a dislocated shoulder, another an abscess, a third a fistula, a fourth the headache. And am I, then, to sit uttering pretty trifling thoughts and little exclamations that, when you have praised me, you may each of you go away with the same dislocated shoulder, the same aching head, the same fistula, and the same abscess that you brought? And is it for this that young men are to travel? And do they leave their parents, their friends, their relations, and their estates that they may praise you while you are uttering little exclamations?

E. D. iii. 24, 2.

Un ℗

UP and down, from one age to another, go the ordinary things of the world, being still the same   And either of every thing in particular before it come to pass, the mind of the Universe doth consider with itself and deliberate : (and if so, then submit for shame unto the determination of such an excellent Understanding) · or once for all it did resolve upon all things in general ; and since that, whatsoever happens, happens by a necessary consequence, and all things indivisibly in a manner and inseparably hold one of another. In sum, either there is a God, and then all is well , or if all things go by chance and fortune, yet must thou use thine own providence in those things that concern thee properly , and then art thou well.

M. A. ix. 26.

OF my Grandfather Verus I have learned to be gentle and meek, and to refrain from all anger and passion. From the fame and memory of him that begot me I have learned both shame-fastness and manlike behaviour. Of my Mother I have learned to be religious, and bountiful; and to forbear, not only to do, but to intend any evil; to content myself with a spare diet, and to fly all such excess as is incidental to great wealth. Of my great Grandfather, both to frequent public schools and Auditories, and to get me good and able Teachers at home; and that I ought not to think much, if upon such occasions, I were at excessive charges.

M. A. i. 1.

FROM Claudius Maximus I learnt in all things to endeavour to have power of myself, and in nothing to be carried about ; to be cheerful and courageous in all sudden chances and accidents, as in sicknesses : to love mildness, and moderation, and gravity : and to do my business, whatsoever it be, thoroughly, and without querulousness. Whatsoever he said, all men believed him that as he spake, so he thought, and whatsoever he did, that he did it with a good intent. His manner was, never to wonder at anything; never to be in haste, and yet never slow : nor to be perplexed, or dejected, or at any time unseemly, or excessively to laugh : nor to be angry, or suspicious, but ever ready to do good, and to forgive, and to speak truth ; and all this, as one that seemed rather of himself to have been straight and right, than ever to have been rectified, or redressed : neither was there any man that ever thought himself undervalued by him, or that could find in his heart, to think himself a better man than he. He would also be very pleasant and gracious.

M. A. i. 12.

NOTHING is meaner than the love of pleasure, the love of gain, and insolence. Nothing is nobler than magnanimity, meekness, and good-nature

E. FR. 46.

IN my Father, I observed his meekness, his constancy without wavering in those things, which after a due examination and deliberation, he had determined. How free from all vanity he carried himself in matter of honour and dignity, (as they are esteemed:) his laboriousness, and assiduity, his readiness to hear any man, that had aught to say, tending to any common good. how generally and impartially he would give every man his due; his skill and knowledge, when rigour or extremity, or when remissness or moderation was in season.

M. A. i. 13.

Un   ⒶR

DO all things as becometh the Disciple of
Antoninus Pius. Remember his resolute
constancy in things that were done by him according to reason, his equability in all things, his
sanctity; the cheerfulness of his countenance,
his sweetness, and how free he was from all
vainglory; how careful to come to the true and
exact knowledge of matters in hand, and how he
would by no means give over till he did fully
and plainly understand the whole state of the
business; and how patiently, and without any
contestation he would bear with them, that did
unjustly condemn him: how he would never be
overhasty in anything, nor give ear to slanders
and false accusations, but examine and observe
with best diligence the several actions and dispositions of men. Again, how he was no back-
biter, nor easily frighted, nor suspicious, and in
his language free from all affectation and curiosity:
and how easily he would content himself with
few things, as lodging, bedding, clothing, and
ordinary nourishment, and attendance. How
able to endure labour, how patient: his uniformity
and constancy in matter of friendship. How he
would bear with them that with all boldness and
liberty opposed his opinions, and even rejoice
if any man could better advise him : and lastly,
how religious he was without superstition. All
these things of him remember, that whensoever
thy last hour shall come upon thee, it may find
thee, as it did him, ready for it in the possession
of a good conscience.

M. A. vi. 28.

IF thou shalt find anything in this mortal life better than righteousness, than truth, temperance, fortitude, and in general better than a mind contented both with those things which according to right and reason she doth, and in those, which without her will and knowledge happen unto thee by the Providence : If I say, thou canst find out anything better than this; apply thyself unto it with thy whole heart.

M. A. iii. 7.

BUT who ever came into the world without an innate idea of good and evil, fair and base, becoming and unbecoming, happiness and misery, proper and improper, what ought to be done and what not to be done?

E. D. ii. 11, 1.

WHENEVER, therefore, anyone makes his interest to consist in the same thing with sanctity, virtue, his country, parents, and friends, all these are secured; but wherever they are made to interfere, friends, and country, and family, and justice itself, all give way, borne down by the weight of self-interest. For wherever *I* and *mine* are placed, thither must every animal gravitate. If in body, that will sway us; if in choice, that; if in externals, these. If, therefore, I be placed in a right choice, then only I shall be a friend, a son, or a father, such as I ought. For in that case it will be for my interest to preserve the faithful, the modest, the patient, the abstinent, the beneficent character; to keep the relations of life inviolate. But, if I place myself in one thing, and virtue in another, the doctrine of Epicurus will stand its ground, That virtue is nothing, or mere opinion.

E. D. ii. 22, 2.

DIFFICULTIES are the things that show what men are. For the future, on any difficulty, remember that God, like a master of exercise, has engaged you with a rough antagonist.

For what end?

That you may be a conqueror like one in the Olympic games, and it cannot be without toil. No man, in my opinion, has a more advantageous difficulty on his hands than you have; provided you will but use it as an athletic champion doth his antagonist.

E. D. i. 24, I.

Un   ®

WHAT, then, ought each of us to say upon every difficult occasion? "It was for this that I exercised, it was for this that I prepared myself." God says to you, Give me a proof if you have gone through the preparatory combats, according to rule; if you have followed a proper diet, a proper exercise; if you have obeyed your master; and after this, do you faint at the very time of action? Now is the proper time for a fever—bear it well; for thirst, bear it well; for hunger, bear it well. Is it not in your power? Who shall restrain you? A physician may restrain you from drinking, but he cannot restrain you from bearing your thirst well. He may restrain you from eating, but he cannot restrain you from bearing hunger well.—But I cannot follow my studies.—And for what end do you follow them, wretch? Is it not that you may be prosperous? That you may be constant? That you may think and act conformably to nature? What restrains you, but that in a fever you may preserve your ruling faculty conformable to nature? Here is the proof of the matter. Here is the trial of the philosopher; for a fever is a part of life, just as a walk, a voyage, or a journey.

E. D. iii. 10.

I AM persuaded there must be someone among
you who sit here that feels secret pangs of
impatience, and says: "When will such a difficulty
come to my share as hath now fallen to his?
Must I sit wasting my life in a corner when I
might be crowned at Olympia? When will anyone bring the news of such a combat for me?"
Such should be the disposition of you all. Even
among the gladiators of Cæsar there are some who
bear it very ill, that they are not brought upon the
stage and matched; and who offer vows to God,
and address the officers, begging to fight. And
will none among you appear such? I would
willingly take a voyage on purpose to see how a
champion of mine acts; how he treats his subject.
"I do not choose such a subject," say you. Is it
in your power, then, to take what subject you
choose? Such a body is given you; such
parents, such brothers, such a country, and such
a rank in it; and then you come to me and
say: "Change my subject." Besides, have not
you abilities to manage that which is given you?

E. D. i. 29, 6.

FEBRUARY I

PRAY, what would Hercules have been if he had said "What can be done to prevent a great lion or a great boar or savage men from coming in my way?" Why, what is that to you? If a great boar should come in your way, you will fight the greater combat; if wicked men, you will deliver the world from wicked men.—"But, then, if I should die by this means?"—You will die a good man in the performance of a gallant action.

E. D. iv. 9, 2.

CONDEMN your actions: but when you have condemned them, do not despair of yourself, nor be like those poor-spirited people who, when they have once given way, abandon themselves entirely, and are carried along as by a torrent. Take example from the wrestling masters. Hath the boy fallen down? Get up again, they say; wrestle again till you have acquired strength.

E. D. iv. 9, 2.

32

PRAY, what figure do you think Hercules would have made if there had not been such a lion, and a hydra, and a stag, and unjust and brutal men; whom he expelled and cleared away? And what would he have done if none of these had existed? Is it not plain that he must have wrapped himself up and slept? In the first place, then, he would never have become a Hercules by slumbering away his whole life in such delicacy and ease; or if he had, what good would it have done? What would have been the use of his arm, and the rest of his strength; of his patience, and greatness of mind, if such circumstances and subjects of action had not roused and exercised him?

What then: must we provide these things for ourselves, and introduce a boar, and a lion, and a hydra, into our country?

This would be madness and folly. But as they were in being, and to be met with, they were proper subjects to set off and exercise Hercules. Do you therefore likewise, being sensible of this, inspect the faculties you have, and after taking a view of them, say, "Bring on me now, O Jupiter, what difficulty thou wilt, for I have faculties granted me by thee, and abilities by which I may acquire honour and ornament to myself."—No; but you sit trembling, for fear this or that should happen; and lamenting, and mourning, and groaning at what doth happen; and then you accuse the gods.

E. D. i. 6, 6.

THE first and highest purity, or impurity, then, is that which is formed in the soul. But you will not find the impurity of the soul and body to be alike. For what else of impurity can you find in the soul than that which renders it filthy with regard to its operations? Now the operations of the soul are its pursuits and avoidances, its desires, aversions, preparations, intentions, assents. What, then, is that which renders it defiled and impure in these operations? Nothing else than its perverse judgments. So that the impurity of the soul consists in wicked principles, and its purification in the forming right principles; and that is pure which hath right principles, for that alone is unmixed and undefiled in its operations.

E. D. iv. 10, 2.

34

Un   ℝ

NEVER esteem of anything as profitable, which shall ever constrain thee either to break thy faith, or to lose thy modesty; to hate any man, to suspect, to curse, to dissemble, to lust after anything that requireth the secret of walls, or veils. But he that preferreth before all things his Rational part and Spirit, and the sacred mysteries of virtue which issueth from it, he shall never lament and exclaim, never sigh, he shall never want either solitude or company: and which is chiefest of all, he shall live without either desire or fear. And as for life, whether for a long or short time he shall enjoy his soul thus compassed about with a body, he is altogether indifferent. For if even now he were to depart, he is as ready for it, as for any other action, which may be performed with modesty, and decency. For all his life long, this is his only care, that his mind may always be occupied in such intentions and objects, as are proper to a rational sociable creature.

E. D. iii. 8.

DO men lose nothing but money? Is not modesty to be lost? Is not decency to be lost? Or may he who loses these suffer no damage? You, indeed, perhaps no longer think anything of this sort to be a damage. But there was once a time when you accounted this to be the only damage and hurt; when you were anxiously afraid lest anyone should shake your regard from these discourses and actions. See, it is not shaken by another, but by yourself. Fight against yourself, recover yourself to decency, to modesty, to freedom.

E. D. iv. 9, 2.

DO not variegate the structure of your walls with Eubœan and Spartan stone; but adorn both the minds of the citizens and of those who govern them by the Grecian education. For cities are made good habitations by the sentiments of those who live in them, not by wood and stone.

E. FR. 77.

36

WHAT doth an adulterer lose? The modest, the chaste character; the neighbour. What doth an angry person lose? Something else. A coward? Something else. No one is wicked without some loss or damage. Now, if, after all, you make the loss of money the only damage, all these are unhurt and undamaged. Nay, it may be, even gainers; as, by such practices, their money may possibly be increased. But consider: if you refer everything to money, the man who loses his nose is not hurt. Yea, say you, he is maimed in his body. Well; but doth he, who loses his smell itself, lose nothing? Is there, then, no faculty of the soul which he who possesses it is the better for, and he who parts with it the worse?

What sort do you mean?

Have we not a natural sense of honour?

We have.

Doth he who loses this suffer no damage? Is he deprived of nothing? Doth he part with nothing that belongs to him? Have we no natural fidelity? No natural affection? No natural disposition to mutual usefulness, to mutual forbearance? Is he, then, who carelessly suffers himself to be damaged in these respects, unhurt and undamaged?

E. D. II 10, 5.

KEEP thyself pure from all violent passion, and evil affection, from all rashness and vanity, and from all manner of discontent, either in regard of the gods, or men. For indeed whatsoever proceeds from the gods, deserves respect for their worth and excellency ; and whatsoever proceeds from men, as they are our kinsmen, should by us be entertained, with love, always ; sometimes, as proceeding from their ignorance of that which is truly good and bad (a blindness no less, than that by which we are not able to discern between white and black) with a kind of pity and compassion also.

M. Λ. ii. 11.

IT is high time for thee to understand that there is somewhat in thee, better and more divine than either thy passions, or thy sensual appetites and affections. What is now the object of my mind, is it fear, or suspicion, or lust, or any such thing? To do nothing rashly without some certain end; let that be thy first care. The next, to have no other end than the common good. For, alas! yet a little while, and thou art no more: no more will any, either of those things that now thou seest, or of those men that now are living, be any more.

M. A. xii 15.

39

Un ®

UPON every action that thou art about, put this question to thyself; How will this when it is done agree with me? Shall I have no occasion to repent of it? Yet a very little while and I am dead and gone; and all things are at end. What then do I care for more than this, that my present action, whatsoever it be, may be the proper action of one that is reasonable; whose end is, the common good; who in all things is ruled and governed by the same law of right and reason, by which God Himself is.

M. A. viii. 2.

CONTRACT thy whole life to the measure and proportion of one single action. And if in every particular action thou dost perform what is fitting to the utmost of thy power, let it suffice thee. And who can hinder thee, but that thou mayest perform what is fitting? But there may be some outward let and impediment. Not any, that can hinder thee, but that whatsoever thou doest, thou may do it, justly, temperately, and with the praise of God. Yea, but there may be somewhat, whereby some operation or other of thine may be hindered. And then, with that very thing that doth hinder, thou mayest be well pleased, and so by this gentle and æquanimous conversion of thy mind unto that which may be, instead of that which at first thou didst intend, in the room of that former action there succeedeth another, which agrees as well with this contraction of thy life, that we now speak of.

M. A. viii. 3.

WHERE is improvement, then?
If any of you, withdrawing himself from externals, turns to his own faculty of choice, to exercise, and finish, and render it conformable to nature; elevated, free, unrestrained, unhindered, faithful, decent: if he hath learnt too, that whoever desires, or is averse to, things out of his own power, can neither be faithful nor free, but must necessarily be changed and tossed up and down with them; must necessarily too be subject to others, to such as can procure or prevent what he desires or is averse to: if, rising in the morning, he observes and keeps to these rules; bathes and eats as a man of fidelity and honour, and thus, on every subject of action, exercises himself in his principal duty; as a racer, in the business of racing; as a public speaker, in the business of exercising his voice: this is he who truly improves; this is he who hath not wrought in vain.

E. D. i. 4, 4.

Un   · ®

WHEN you let go your attention for a little while, do not fancy you may recover it whenever you please; but remember this, that by means of the fault of to-day your affairs must necessarily be in a worse condition for the future. First, what is the saddest thing of all, a habit arises of not attending; and then a habit of deferring the attention, and always driving off from time to time, and procrastinating a prosperous life, a propriety of behaviour, and the thinking and acting conformably to nature. Now, if the procrastination of anything is advantageous, the absolute omission of it is still more advantageous; but, if it be not advantageous, why do not you preserve a constant attention?

E. D. iv. 12, 1.

" WHAT, then, is it possible by these means to be faultless?" Impracticable, but this is possible, to use a constant endeavour to be faultless. For we shall have cause to be satisfied if, by never remitting this attention, we shall be exempt at least from a few faults.

E. D. iv. 12, 4.

42

TWO things must be rooted out of man : conceit and diffidence. Conceit lies in thinking you want nothing; and diffidence, in supposing it impossible, that under such adverse circumstances, you should succeed.

E. D. iii. 14, 4.

WHAT, then, is it to be properly educated? To learn how to adapt natural preconceptions to particular cases, conformably to nature ; and, for the future, to distinguish that some things are in our own power, others not. In our own power are choice, and all actions dependent on choice; not in our power, the body, the parts of the body, property, parents, brothers, children, country, and, in short, all with whom we are engaged in society. Where, then, shall we place good? To what kind of things shall we adapt the preconception of it? To that in our own power.

E. D. i. 22, 2.

IT is not easy to gain the attention of effeminate young men, for you cannot take custard by a hook; but the ingenuous, even if you discourage them, are the more eager for learning. Hence Rufus, for the most part, did discourage them, and made use of that as a criterion of the ingenuous and disingenuous. For he used to say, As a stone, even if you throw it up, will by its own propensity be carried downward; so an ingenuous mind, the more it is forced from its natural bent, the more strongly will it incline towards it.

E. D. iii. 6, 4.

WHATEVER rules you have deliberately proposed to yourself for the conduct of life, abide by them as so many laws, and as if you would be guilty of impiety in transgressing any of them; and do not regard what anyone says of you, for this, after all, is no concern of yours.

E. M. 50.

IF you perceive any of those things which you have learned and studied occurring to you in action, rejoice in them. If you have laid aside ill-nature and reviling; if you have lessened your harshness, indecent language, inconsiderateness, effeminacy; if you are not moved by the same things as formerly, if not in the same manner as formerly, you may keep a perpetual festival: to-day, because you have behaved well in one affair; to-morrow, because in another. How much better a reason for sacrifice is this, than obtaining a consulship or a government?

E. D. iv. 4, 5.

WHENSOEVER by some present hard occurrences thou art constrained to be in some sort troubled and vexed, return unto thyself as soon as may be, and be not out of tune longer than thou must needs. For so shalt thou be the better able to keep thy part another time, and to maintain the harmony, if thou dost use thyself to this continually; once out, presently to have recourse unto it. and to begin again.

M. A. vi. 9.

Un   ⓡ

IT is not death or pain that is to be feared; but the fear of pain or death. Hence we commend him who says:

> Death is no ill, but shamefully to die.

Courage, then, ought to be opposed to death, and caution to the fear of death: whereas we, on the contrary, oppose to death, flight; and to our principle concerning it, carelessness and desperateness and indifference.

E. D. ii. 1, 2.

THE materials of action are indifferent; but the use of them is not indifferent.

How, then, shall one preserve intrepidity and tranquillity; and at the same time be careful, and neither rash nor indolent?

By imitating those who play at tables. The dice are indifferent; the pieces are indifferent. How do I know what will fall out? But it is my business to manage carefully and dexterously whatever doth fall out. Thus in life, too, this is the chief business; distinguish and separate things, and say, "Externals are not in my power, choice is. Where shall I seek good and evil? Within; in what is my own." But in what belongs to others, call nothing good, or evil, or profit, or hurt, or anything of that sort.

E. D. ii. 5, 1.

Un   ℝ

HERE is the artificer; here are the materials; what is it we want? Is not the thing capable of being taught? It is. Is it not in our own power, then? The only thing of all others that is so. Neither riches, nor health, nor fame, nor, in short, anything else, is in our power, except the right use of the appearances of things. This alone is, by nature, not subject to restraint, not subject to hindrance. Why, then, do not you finish it? Tell me the cause. It must be by my fault, or yours, or from the nature of the thing. The thing itself is practicable, and the only one in our power. The fault then must be either in me, or in you, or, more truly, in both. Well, then, shall we now, at last, bring this intention along with us? Let us lay aside all that is past. Let us begin. Only believe me, and you will see the consequence.

E. D. ii. 19, 4.

48

ALL are preserved and improved by operations correspondent to their several faculties; as a carpenter, by building; a grammarian, by grammar; but if he accustom himself to write ungrammatically, his art will necessarily be spoiled and destroyed. Thus modest actions preserve the modest man, and immodest ones destroy him; faithful actions, the faithful man, and the contrary destroy him. On the other hand, contrary actions heighten contrary characters. Thus impudence, an impudent one; knavery, a knavish one; slander, a slanderous one, anger, an angry one; and inequitable dealings, a covetous one.

E. D. ii. 9, 2.

HOW do we act in a voyage? What is in my power? To choose the pilot, the sailors, the day, the time of day. Afterwards comes a storm. What have I to care for? My part is performed. The subject belongs to another, to the pilot. But the ship is sinking: what then have I to do? That which alone I can do; I am drowned, without fear, without clamour, or accusing God; but as one who knows that what is born must likewise die. For I am not eternity, but a man; a part of the whole, as an hour is of the day. I must come like an hour, and like an hour must pass away. What signifies it whether by drowning or by a fever? For, in some way or other, pass I must.

E. D. ii. 5, 2.

YOU see that Cæsar hath procured us a profound peace; there are neither wars nor battles, nor great robberies nor piracies, but we may travel at all hours, and sail from east to west. But can Cæsar procure us peace from a fever too? From a shipwreck? From a fire? From an earthquake? From a thunderstorm? Nay, even from love? He cannot. From grief? From envy? No, not from any one of these. But the doctrine of philosophers promises to procure us peace from these too. And what doth it say? "If you will attend to me, O mortals, wherever you are, and whatever you are doing, you shall neither grieve nor be angry, nor be compelled nor restrained; but you shall live impassive, and free from all." Shall not he who enjoys this peace, proclaimed, not by Cæsar (for how should he have it to proclaim?) but by God, through reason, be contented, when he is alone reflecting and considering: "To me there can now no ill happen; there is no thief, no earthquake. All is full of peace, all full of tranquillity; every road, every city, every assembly. My neighbour, my companion, unable to hurt me."

E. D. iii. 13, 1.

EVERY error in life implies a contradiction . for, since he who errs doth not mean to err, but to be in the right, it is evident that he acts contrary to his meaning. What doth a thief mean? His own interest. If, then, thieving be against his interest, he acts contrary to his own meaning. Now every rational soul is naturally averse to self-contradiction but so long as anyone is ignorant that it is a contradiction, nothing restrains him from acting contradictorily: but whenever he discovers it, he must as necessarily renounce and avoid it, as anyone must dissent from a falsehood whenever he perceives it to be a falsehood : but while this doth not appear, he assents to it as to a truth.

E. D. ii. 26, 1.

THIS, again, is folly and insolence to say: "I am impassive and undisturbed. Be it known to you, mortals, that while you are fluctuating and bustling about for things of no value, I alone am free from all perturbation."—Are you then so far from being contented with having no pain yourself, that you must needs make proclamation: "Come hither, all you who have the gout, or the headache, or a fever, or are lame, or blind, and see me free from every distemper." This is vain and shocking, unless you could show, like Æsculapius, by what method of cure they may presently become as free from distempers as yourself, and bring your own health as a proof of it.

E. D. iv. 3, 5.

WHEN one of the company said to him, "Convince me that logic is necessary."

"Would you have me demonstrate it to you?" says he.

"Yes."

"Then I must use a demonstrative form of argument."

"Granted."

"And how will you know then whether I argue sophistically?"

On this, the man being silent,

"You see," says he, "that even by your own confession, logic is necessary; since without its assistance, you cannot learn so much as whether it be necessary or not."

E. D. ii. 25.

WHAT is asserted by the philosophers may, perhaps, appear a paradox to some : let us, however, examine, as well as we can, whether this be true. That it is possible in all things to act at once with caution and courage. For caution seems, in some measure, contrary to courage; and contraries are by no means consistent. The appearance of a paradox to many, in the present case, seems to me to arise from something like this. If, indeed, we assert that courage and caution are to be used in the same instances, we should justly be accused of uniting contradictions: but, in the way that we affirm it, where is the absurdity? For, if what hath been so often said, and so often demonstrated, be certain, that the essence of good and evil consists in the use of the appearances; and that things independent on choice are not of the nature either of good or evil: what paradox do the philosophers assert, if they say : "Where things are not dependent on choice, be courageous; where they are, be cautious?" For in these only, if evil consists in a bad choice, is caution to be used.

E. D. ii. 1, 1.

Un   · ®

SET death before me, set pain, set a prison, set
ignomony, set condemnation before me, and
you will know me. This is the proper ostentation of a young man come out from the schools.
Leave the rest to others. Let no one ever hear
you utter a word about them, nor suffer it, if anyone commends you for them : but think that you
are nobody, and that you know nothing. Appear
to know only this, how you may never be disappointed of your desire ; never incur your aversion. Let others study causes, problems, and
syllogisms. Do you study death, chains, torture,
exile : and all these with courage, and reliance
upon him who hath called you to them, and
judged you worthy a post in which you may
show what the rational governing faculty can do
when set in array against powers independent
on the choice. And thus, this paradox becomes
neither impossible nor a paradox, that we must
be at once cautious and courageous : courageous
in what doth not depend upon choice, and
cautious in what doth.

E. D. ii. 1, 5.

H E that hath not one and the selfsame general end always as long as he liveth, cannot possibly be one and the selfsame man always. But this will not suffice except thou add also what ought to be this general end. For as the general conceit and apprehension of all those things which upon no certain ground are by the greater part of men deemed good, cannot be uniform and agreeable, but that only which is limited, and restrained by some certain proprieties and conditions, as of community : that nothing be conceived good, which is not commonly, and publicly good : so must the end also that we propose unto ourselves, be common and sociable. For he that doth direct all his own private motions and purposes to that end, all his actions will be agreeable and uniform , and by that means will be still the same man.

M. A. xi. 19.

L ET it always appear, and be manifest unto thee, that solitariness, and desert places, by many Philosophers, so much esteemed of, and affected, are of themselves but thus and thus ; and that all things are here to them that live in Towns, and converse with others . as they are the same nature everywhere to be seen and observed : to them that have retired themselves to the top of mountains, and to desert Havens, or what other desert and inhabited places soever. For anywhere if thou wilt mayest thou quickly find and apply that to thyself, which Plato saith of his Philosopher, in a place ; as private and retired saith he, as if he were shut up and enclosed about in some Shepherd's lodge, on the top of a hill. There by thyself to put these questions to thyself, or to enter into these considerations : What is my chief and principal part, which hath power over the rest ? What is now the present estate of it, as I use it ; and what is it, that I employ it about ? Is it now void of reason or no ? Is it free, and separated ; or so affixed, so congealed and grown together, as it were with the flesh, that it is swayed by the motions and inclinations of it ?

M. A. x. 24.

SOLITUDE is the state of a helpless person. For not he who is alone is therefore solitary, any more than one in a crowd the contrary. When therefore, we lose a son, or a brother, or a friend on whom we have been used to repose, we often say we are left solitary even in the midst of Rome, where such a crowd is continually meeting us.

E. D. iii. 13, 1.

AT what time soever thou wilt, it is in thy power, to retire into thyself, and to be at rest, and free from all businesses. A man cannot any-whither retire better, than to his own soul: he especially who is beforehand provided of such things within, which whensoever he doth with-draw himself to look in, may presently afford unto him perfect ease and tranquillity.

M. A. iv. 3.

A T thy first encounter with anyone, say presently to thyself; This man, what are his
opinions concerning that which is good or evil?
as concerning pain, pleasure, and the causes of
both; concerning honour, and dishonour, concerning life and death; thus and thus. Now if
it be no wonder that a man should have such and
such opinions, how can it be a wonder that he
should do such and such things ?   I will remember
then, that he cannot but do as he doth holding
those opinions that he doth.   Remember, that as
it is a shame for any man to wonder that a fig-
tree should bear figs, so also to wonder that the
World should bear anything, whatsoever it is
which in the ordinary course of nature it may
bear.   To a physician also and to a pilot it is
a shame either for the one to wonder, that such
and such a one should have an ague ; or for the
other, that the winds should prove contrary.

M. A. viii. 13.

MARCH I

THOU must continually ponder and consider
with thyself, what manner of men they be,
and for their minds and understandings what is
their present estate, whose good word and testimony thou dost desire.   For then neither wilt
thou see cause to complain of them that offend
against their wills; or find any want of their
applause, if once thou dost but penetrate into
the true force and ground both of their opinions,
and of their desires.   "No soul (saith he) is
willingly bereaved of the Truth," and by consequence, neither of justice, or temperance, or kindness, and mildness, nor of anything that is of
the same kind. It is most needful that thou
shouldst always remember this.   For so shalt
thou be far more gentle and moderate towards
all men.

M. A. vii. 34.

THEY that shall oppose thee in thy right courses, as it is not in their power to divert thee from thy good action, so neither let it be to divert thee from thy good affection towards them. But be it thy care to keep thyself constant in both; both in a right judgment and action, and in true meekness towards them, that either shall do their endeavour to hinder thee, or at least will be displeased with thee for what thou hast done. For to fail in either (either in the one to give over for fear, or in the other to forsake thy natural affection towards him, who by nature is both thy friend and thy kinsman) is equally base, and much savouring of the disposition of a cowardly fugitive soldier.

M A. xi. 8.

LABOUR not as one to whom it is appointed to be wretched, nor as one that either would be pitied, or admired; but let this be thine only care and desire; so always and in all things to prosecute or to forbear, as the law of Charity, or mutual society doth require.

M. A. ix. 10.

HAVE I done anything charitably? then am I benefited by it. See that this upon all occasions may present itself unto thy mind, and never cease to think of it. What is thy profession? to be good.

M. A. xi. 4.

WHAT wouldst thou have more? Unto him that is a man, thou hast done a good turn: doth not that suffice thee? Must thou be rewarded for it?

M. A. ix. 43.

TO them that ask thee, Where hast thou seen the Gods, or how knowest thou certainly that there be Gods, that thou art so devout in their worship? I answer first of all, that even to the very eye, they are in some manner visible and apparent. Secondly, neither have I ever seen mine own soul, and yet I respect and honour it. So then for the Gods, by the daily experience that I have of their power and providence towards myself and others, I know certainly that they are, and therefore worship them.

M. A. xii. 21.

THOU shalt find it a very good help, to remember the Gods as often as may be; and that, the thing which they require at our hands, of as many of us, as are by nature reasonable creatures; is not that with fair words, and outward show of piety and devotion we should flatter them, but that we should become like unto them.

M. A. x 8.

BUT gods there be certainly, and they take care for the world; and as for those things which be truly evil, as vice and wickedness, such things they have put in a man's own power, that he might avoid them if he would: and had there been anything besides that had been truly bad and evil, they would have had a care of that also, that a man might have avoided it. But why should that be thought to hurt and prejudice a man's life in this world, which cannot anywise make man himself the better, or the worse in his own person? Neither must we think that the Nature of the Universe did either through ignorance pass these things, or if not as ignorant of them, yet as unable either to prevent, or better to order and dispose them. It cannot be that she through want either of power or skill, should have committed such a thing, so as to suffer all things both good and bad, equally and promiscuously to happen unto all both good and bad. As for life therefore, and death, honour and dishonour, labour and pleasure, riches and poverty, all these things happen unto men indeed, both good and bad, equally; but as things which of themselves are neither good nor bad; because of themselves, neither shameful nor praiseworthy.

M. A. ii. 8.

Un ℞

THINK oftener of God than you breathe.

E. FR. 114.

ARE not the gods everywhere at the same distance? Do not they everywhere equally see what is doing?

E. D iv. 4, 5.

HE liveth with the gods, who at all times affords unto them the spectacle of a soul both contented and well pleased with whatsoever is afforded or allotted unto her; and performing whatsoever is pleasing to that spirit whom (being part of himself) Zeus hath appointed to every man as his overseer and governor.

M. A. 5, 21.

IF you always remember that God stands by, an inspector of whatever you do either in soul or body, you will never err, either in your prayers or actions, and you will have God abiding with you.

E. FR. 115.

66

EITHER the Gods can do nothing for us at all, or they can still and allay all the distractions and distempers of thy mind. If they can do nothing, why dost thou pray? If they can, why wouldst not thou rather pray, that they will grant unto thee, that thou mayest neither fear, nor lust after any of those worldly things which cause these distractions, and distempers of it? Why not rather, that thou mayest not at either their absence or presence, be grieved and discontented: than either that thou mayest obtain them, or that thou mayest avoid them? For certainly it must needs be, that if the Gods can help us in anything, they may in this kind also. But thou wilt say perchance, In those things the Gods have given me my liberty: and it is in mine own power to do what I will. But if thou mayest use this liberty, rather to set thy mind at true liberty, than wilfully with baseness and servility of mind, to affect those things, which either to compass or to avoid is not in thy power, wert not thou better? And as for the Gods. who hath told thee, that they may not help us up even in those things that they have put in our own power? Whether it be so or no, thou shalt soon perceive, if thou wilt but try thyself and pray.

M. A. xi. 40.

GOD beholds our minds and understandings, bare and naked from these material vessels, and outsides, and all earthly dross. For with His simple and pure understanding, He pierceth into our inmost and purest parts, which from His, as it were by a water pipe and channel, first flowed and issued.

M. A. xii. 2.

LET thy god that is in thee to rule over thee, find by thee, that he hath to do with a man, that hath ordered his life, as one that expecteth, as it were, nothing but the sound of the trumpet, sounding a retreat to depart out of this life with all expedition.

M A iii. 5.

WHENEVER you lay anything to the charge of Providence, do but reflect, and you will find that it hath happened agreeably to reason.

Well, but a dishonest man hath the advantage.

In what ?

In money.

Why, he is better qualified for it than you; because he flatters, he throws away shame, he keeps awake; and where is the wonder? But look whether he hath the advantage of you in fidelity or in honour. You will find he hath not; but that wherever it is best for you to have advantage of him, there you have it.

E. D. iii. 17, 1.

REMEMBER, that all things in general are by certain order and appointment.

M. A. vii. 22.

Un   ·Ⓡ

H OW comes it to pass, that the Gods having ordered all other things so well and so lovingly, should be overseen in this one only thing, that whereas there hath been some very good men, that have made many covenants as it were with God, and by many holy actions, and outward services contracted a kind of familiarity with Him, that these men when once they are dead, should never be restored to life, but be extinct for ever. But this thou mayest be sure of, that this (if it be so indeed) would never have been so ordered by the Gods, had it been fit otherwise.

M. A. xii. 4.

C AN the gods, who are immortal, for the continuance of so many ages bear without indignation with such and so many sinners, as have ever been, yea not only so, but also take such care for them, that they want nothing; and dost thou so grievously take on, as one that could bear with them no longer; thou that art but for a moment of time? yea thou that art one of those sinners thyself?

M. A. vii. 41.

HAVE no will but the will of God; and who shall restrain you, who shall compel you any more than God? When you have such a guide, and conform your will and inclinations to his, what need you fear being disappointed? Yield up your desire and aversion to riches, or poverty; the one will be disappointed, the other incurred. Yield them up to health, power, honours, your country, friends, children, in short, to anything independent on choice, you will be unfortunate. But yield them up to Jupiter and the other gods. Give yourself up to these; let these govern, let both be ranged on the same side with these; and how can you be any longer unprosperous? But if, poor wretch, you envy, and pity, and are jealous, and tremble, and never cease a single day from complaining of yourself and the Gods, why do you boast of your education?

E. D. ii. 17, 1.

.

EITHER this Universe is a mere confused mass, and an intricate context of things, which shall in time be scattered and dispersed again : or it is an Union consisting of Order, and administered by providence. If the first, why should I desire to continue any longer in this for- tuitous confusion and commixtion ? or why should I take care for anything else, but that as soon as may be I may be Earth again ? And why should I trouble myself any more whilst I seek to please the gods? Whatsoever I do, Dispersion is my end, and will come upon me whether I will or no. But if the latter be, then am not I religious in vain ; then will I be quiet and patient, and put my trust in Him, who is the governor of all.

M. A. vi. 8

.

Un   ' ®

EITHER Fate, (and that either an absolute necessity, and unavoidable decree; or a placable and flexible Providence) or All is a mere casual Confusion, void of all order and government. If an absolute and unavoidable Necessity, why dost thou resist? If a placable and exorable Providence, make thyself worthy of the divine help and assistance. If all be a mere confusion without any Moderator, or Governor, then hast thou reason to congratulate thyself, that in such a general flood of Confusion, thou thyself hast obtained a reasonable Faculty, whereby thou mayest govern thine own life and actions.

M. A. xii. 11.

Un   ®

CONSIDER the exertions of God's power, and His administration. What hath He given me, my own, and independent? What hath He reserved to Himself? He hath given me whatever depends upon choice. The things in my power He hath made incapable of hindrance or restraint. But how could He make a body of clay incapable of hindrance? Therefore He hath subjected possessions, furniture, house, children, wife, to the revolution of the universe. Why, then, do I fight against God? Why do I will to retain what depends not on will? What is not granted absolutely; but how? In such a manner and for such a time as was thought proper But He who gave, takes away. Why, then, do I resist? Not to say that I shall be a fool in contending with a stronger than myself; what is a prior consideration, I shall be unjust. For whence had I these things when I came into the world? My father gave them to me. And who gave them to him? And who made the sun? Who the fruits? Who the seasons? Who their connection and relation to each other? And, after you have received all, and even your very self, from another, are you angry with the giver, and complain if he takes anything away from you?

E. D. IV 1, 12

IF we had any understanding, ought we not both, in public and in private, incessantly to sing hymns, and speak well of the Deity, and rehearse His benefits? Ought we not, whether we are digging, or ploughing, or eating, to sing the hymn to God? Great is God, who has supplied us with these instruments to till the ground : great is God, who has given us hands, a power of swallowing, a stomach : who has given us to grow insensibly, to breathe in sleep. Even these things we ought upon every occasion to celebrate ; but to make it the subject of the greatest and most divine hymn, that He has given us the faculty of apprehending them, and using them in a proper way. Well then : because the most of you are blind and insensible, was it not necessary that there should be someone to fill this station, and give out, for all men, the hymn to God? For what else can I, a lame old man, do but sing hymns to God? If I was a nightingale, I would act the part of a nightingale : if a swan, the part of a swan. But, since I am a reasonable creature, it is my duty to praise God. This is my business. I do it. Nor will I ever desert this post as long as it is vouchsafed me ; and I exhort you to join in the same song.

E. D. i. 16, 2.

BE assured that the essential property of piety towards the gods is to form right opinions concerning them, as existing and as governing the universe with goodness and justice. And fix yourself in this resolution, to obey them, and yield to them, and willingly follow them in all events, as produced by the most perfect understanding. For thus you will never find fault with the gods, nor accuse them as neglecting you.

E. M. 31.

IT is better to die with hunger, exempt from grief and fear, than to live in affluence with perturbation; and it is better your servant should be bad, than you unhappy.

Begin therefore from little things. Is a little oil spilt? a little wine stolen? Say to yourself, "This is the purchase paid for tranquillity, and nothing is to be had for nothing."

E. M. 12.

I HAVE ranged my pursuits under the direction of God. Is it His will that I should have a fever? It is my will too. Is it His will that I should pursue anything? It is my will too. Is it His will that I should desire? It is my will too. Is it His will that I should obtain anything? It is mine too. Is it not His will? It is not mine. Is it His will that I should be tortured? Then it is my will to be tortured. Is it His will that I should die? Then it is my will to die.

E. D. iv. 1, 12.

HOW is it a paradox to say that when he is whipped or imprisoned or beheaded he is not hurt? If he suffers nobly, doth not he come off even the better, and a gainer? But he is the person hurt who suffers the most miserable and shameful evils; who, instead of a man, becomes a wolf or viper or a hornet.

E. D. iv. 1, 13.

IF so be that the gods have deliberated in particular of those things that should happen unto me, I must stand to their deliberation, as discreet and wise. For that a god should be an imprudent god, is a thing hard even to conceive : and why should they resolve to do me hurt? for what profit either unto them or the universe (which they specially take care for) could arise from it? But if so be that they have not deliberated of me in particular, certainly they have of the whole in general, and those things which in consequence and coherence of this general deliberation happen unto me in particular, I am bound to embrace and accept of. But if so be that they have not deliberated at all (which indeed is very irreligious for any man to believe . for then let us neither sacrifice, nor pray, nor respect our oaths, neither let us any more use any of those things, which we persuaded of the presence and secret conversation of the gods among us, daily use and practise :) but, I say, if so be that they have not indeed either in general, or particular deliberated of any of those things, that happen unto us in this world ; yet God be thanked, that of those things that concern myself, it is lawful for me to deliberate myself.

M. A. vi. 39.

DOTH any good man fear that food should fail him? It doth not fail the blind, it doth not fail the lame. Shall it fail a good man? A paymaster is not wanting to a soldier, or to a labourer, or to a shoemaker, and shall one be wanting to a good man? Is God so negligent of His own institutions, of His servants, of His witnesses, whom alone He makes use of as examples to the uninstructed, both that He is, and that He administers the universe rightly, and doth not neglect human affairs, and that no evil happens to a good man, either living or dead? What, then, is the case when He doth not bestow food? What else than that, like a good general, He hath made me a signal of retreat? I obey, I follow; speaking well of my leader, praising His works. For I came when it seemed good to Him, and again, when it seems' good to Him, I depart; and in life it was my business to praise God, both by myself, to each particular person, and to the world.

E. D. iii. 26, 2.

DO we know, then, what man is? What is his
nature; what our idea of him is; and how
far our ears are open in respect to this matter?
Nay, do you understand what nature is; or are
you able, and in what degree, to comprehend me,
when I come to say, "But I must use demonstration to you"? How should you? Do you comprehend what demonstration is, or how a thing
is demonstrated, or by what methods; or what
resembles a demonstration, and yet is not a demonstration? Do you know what true or false
is? What is consequent to a thing, and what
contradictory? Or unsuitable, or dissonant?

E. D. ii. 24, 1.

BUT I must excite you to philosophy. How shall I show you that contradiction among the generality of mankind, by which they differ concerning good and evil, profitable and unprofitable, when you know not what contradiction means? Show me, then, what I shall gain by discoursing with you. Excite an inclination in me, as a proper pasture excites an inclination to eating in a sheep: for if you offer him a stone, or a piece of bread, he will not be excited. Thus we too have certain natural inclinations to speaking, when the hearer appears to be somebody; when he gives us encouragement; but if he sits by, like a stone or a tuft of grass, how can he excite any desire in a man? Doth a vine say to an husbandman, "Take care of me"? No; but invites him to take care of it, by showing him that if he doth, it will reward him for his care. Who is there whom engaging sprightly children do not invite to play, and creep, and prattle with them? But who was ever taken with an inclination to divert himself, or bray, with an ass? For, be the creature ever so little, it is still a little ass.

E. D. ii. 24, 1.

FIRST, to act as a man. What is comprehended in this? Not to be, though gentle, like a sheep; nor mischievous like a wild beast. But the particular end relates to the study and choice of each individual. A harper is to act as a harper, a carpenter, as a carpenter; a philosopher, as a philosopher; an orator, as an orator. When therefore you say, "Come and hear me read," observe first, not to do this at random, and, in the next place, after you have found to what end you refer it, consider whether it be a proper one. Would you be useful, or be praised? You presently hear him say, "What, do I value the praise of the multitude?" And he says well, for this is nothing to a musician or a geometrician, as such. You would be useful, then. In what? Tell us, that we too may run to make part of your audience. Now, is it possible for anyone to benefit others who hath received no benefit himself? No; for neither can he who is not a carpenter or a shoemaker benefit any in respect to those arts. Would you know, then, whether you have received benefit? Produce your principles, philosopher; what is the aim and promise of desire? Not to be disappointed. What of aversion? Not to be incurred. Come, do we fulfil this promise? Tell me the truth.

E M. iv. 23, 1.

WHAT is man?
A rational and mortal being.

Well: from what are we distinguished by reason?

From wild beasts.

From what else?

From sheep and the like.

Take care, then, to do nothing like a wild beast, otherwise you have destroyed the man; you have not fulfilled what your nature promises. Take care, too, to do nothing like cattle; for thus likewise the man is destroyed.

In what do we act like cattle?

When we act gluttonously, lewdly, rashly, sordidly, inconsiderately, into what are we sunk?

Into cattle.

What have we destroyed?

The rational being.

When we behave contentiously, injuriously, passionately, and violently, into what are we sunk?

Into wild beasts.

And further: some of us are wild beasts of a larger size; others, little mischievous vermin.

E. D. ii. 9, 1, 2.

H ATH God, then, given you eyes in vain? Is it in vain that He hath infused into them such a strong and active spirit as to be able to represent the forms of distant objects? What messenger is so quick and diligent? Is it in vain that He hath made the intermediate air so yielding and elastic that the sight penetrates through it? And is it in vain that He hath made the light, without which all the rest would be useless? Man, be not ungrateful; nor, on the other hand, unmindful of your superior advantages; but for sight and hearing, and indeed for life itself, and the supports of it, as fruits, and wine, and oil, be thankful to God : but remember, that He hath given you another thing, superior to them all : which makes use of them, proves them, estimates the value of each.

E. D. ii. 23, 1.

84

THE true joy of a man is to do that which properly belongs unto a man. That which is most proper unto a man, is First, to be kindly affected towards them, that are of the same kind and nature as he is himself; to contemn all sensual motions and appetites; to discern rightly all plausible fancies and imaginations, to contemplate the nature of the Universe; both it, and all things that are done in it. In which kind of contemplation three several relations are to be observed The first, to the apparent secondary cause. The second, to the first original cause, God, from whom originally proceeds whatsoever doth happen in the world. The third and last, to them that we live and converse with: what use may be made of it, to their use and benefit.

M. A. viii. 25.

E PICURUS knew that, if once a child is born, it is no longer in our power not to love and be solicitous for it. For the same reason, he says, a wise man will not engage himself in public business, for he knew very well what such an engagement would oblige him to do ; for what should restrain anyone from affairs if we may behave among men as we would among a swarm of flies?

And doth he who knows all this dare to bid us not bring up children? Not even a sheep or a wolf deserts its offspring, and shall man? What would you have? That we should be as silly as sheep? Yet even these do not desert their offspring. Or as savage as wolves? Neither do these desert them Pray, who would mind you if he saw his child fallen upon the ground, and crying? For my part, I am of opinion that your father and mother, even if they could have foreseen that you would have been the author of such doctrines, would not, however, have thrown you away.

E. D. i. 23, 1, 2.

WHERE, then, is the great good or evil of man?

Where his difference is. If this is preserved and remains well fortified, and neither honour, fidelity, or judgment is destroyed, then he himself is preserved likewise; but when any of these is lost and demolished, he himself is lost also. In this do all great events consist. Paris, they say, was undone, because the Greeks invaded Troy and laid it waste, and his family were slain in battle. By no means; for no one is undone by an action not his own. All that was only laying waste the nests of storks. But his true undoing was when he lost the modest, the faithful, the hospitable, and the decent character. When was Achilles undone? When Patroclus died? By no means. But when he gave himself up to rage, when he wept over a girl; when he forgot that he came there not to get mistresses, but to fight. This is human undoing; this is the siege; this the overthrow; when right principles are ruined; when these are destroyed.

E. D i. 23, 4.

DIOGENES rightly answered one who desired letters of recommendation from him, "At first sight he will know you to be a man: and whether you are a good or a bad man, if he hath any skill in distinguishing, he will know likewise; and, if he hath not, he will never know it, though I should write a thousand times." Just as if you were a piece of coin, and should desire to be recommended to any person as good, in order to be tried: if it be to an assayer, he will know your value, for you will recommend yourself.

We ought, therefore, in life also, to have something analogous to this skill in gold; that one may be able to say, like the assayer, Bring me whatever piece you will, and I will find out its value. or as I would say with regard to syllogisms, Bring me whoever you will, and I will distinguish for you, whether he knows how to solve syllogisms or not. Why? Because I can solve syllogisms myself, and have that faculty, which is necessary for one who knows how to find out persons skilled in the solution of syllogisms. But how do I act in life? I at some times call a thing good; at others, bad. What is the cause of this? The contrary to what happens in syllogisms: ignorance and inexperience.

E. D. iii. 2, 1, 2.

DO, Soul, do; abuse and contemn thyself; yet a while and the time for thee to respect thyself, will be at an end. Every man's happiness depends upon himself, but behold thy life is almost at an end, whilst affording thyself no respect, thou dost make thy happiness to consist in the souls, and conceits of other men.

Why should any of these things that happen externally, so much distract thee? Give thyself leisure to learn some good thing, and cease roving and wandering to and fro. Thou must also take heed of another kind of wandering, for they are idle in their actions, who toil and labour in this life, and have no certain scope to which to direct all their motions, and desires.

M. A. ii. 3, 4

I F you would appear beautiful, young man, strive
for human excellency.

What is that?

Consider, when you praise without partial
affection, whom you praise : is it the honest, or
the dishonest?

The honest.

The sober or the dissolute?

The sober.

The temperate or the intemperate?

The temperate.

Then, if you make yourself such a character,
you know that you will make yourself beautiful;
but, while you neglect these things, though you
use every contrivance to appear beautiful, you
must necessarily be deformed.

E. D. iii. 1, 1.

IF a person could be persuaded of this principle as he ought, that we are all originally descended from God, and that He is the Father of gods and men, I conceive he never would think meanly or degenerately concerning himself.

E. D. i. 3, 1.

UPON all occasions we ought to have these maxims ready at hand :

> Conduct me, Jove, and thou, O Destiny,
> Wherever your decrees have fixed my station.
> I follow cheerfully ; and, did I not,
> Wicked and wretched, I must follow still.
>
> Whoe'er yields properly to Fate, is deemed
> Wise among men, and knows the laws of heaven.

And this third :

"O Crito, if it thus pleases the gods, thus let it be. Anytus and Meletus may kill me indeed, but hurt me they cannot."

E. M. 52.

APRIL I

IN all vice, pleasure being presented with a bait, draws sensual minds to the hook of perdition.

E. FR. 107.

REPENTANCE, is an inward and self-reprehension for the neglect or omission of somewhat that was profitable. Now whatsoever is good, is also profitable, and it is the part of an honest virtuous man to set by it, and to make reckoning of it accordingly. But never did any honest virtuous man repent of the neglect or omission of any carnal pleasure : no carnal pleasure then is either good or profitable.

M. A. viii. 9.

IT is the character of a wise man to resist pleasure, and of a fool to be enslaved by it.

E. FR. 106.

HAVE the very leaves, and our own bodies, this connection and sympathy with the whole, and have not our souls much more? But our souls are thus connected and intimately joined to God, as being indeed members and distinct portions of His essence.

E. D. i. 14, 1.

GOD hath universally so constituted the nature of every reasonable creature, that no one can attain any of its own proper advantages without contributing something to the use of society.

E. D. i. 19, 2.

SOONER mayest thou find a thing earthly, where no earthly thing is, than find a man that naturally can live by himself alone

M. A. ix. 7.

93

WHATSOEVER I do either by myself, or with some other, the only thing that I must intend, is that it be good and expedient for the public. For as for praise, consider how many who once were much commended, are now already quite forgotten : yea they that commended them, how even they themselves are long since dead and gone.

M. A. vii. 5.

SHOULD I do it? I will: so the end of my action be, to do good unto men. Doth anything by way of cross or adversity happen unto me? I accept it, with reference unto the gods and their providence ; the fountain of all things, from which whatsoever comes to pass doth hang and depend.

M. A. viii. 22

DO not you know what sort of a thing a warfare is? One must keep guard, another go out for a spy, another to battle too. It is neither possible that all should be in the same place, nor, indeed, better: but you, neglecting to perform the orders of your general, complain whenever anything a little hard is commanded, and do not consider what you make the army become as far as lies in your power. For, if all should imitate you, nobody will dig a trench, or throw up a rampart, or watch, or expose himself to danger, but everyone will appear useless to the expedition. Again, if you were a sailor in a voyage, fix upon one place, and there remain. If it should be necessary to climb the mast, refuse to do it; if to run to the head of the ship, refuse to do it. And what captain will bear you? Would not he throw you overboard as a useless piece of goods and mere luggage, and a bad example to the other sailors? Thus, also, in the present case, every one's life is a warfare, and that long and various. You must observe the duty of a soldier, and perform everything at the nod of your general; and even, if possible, divine what he would have done.

E. D. iii. 24, 2.

APRIL 5

A S thou thyself, whoever thou art, wert made
for the perfection and consummation, being
a member of it, of a common society; so must
every action of thine tend to the perfection and
consummation of a life that is truly sociable. What
action soever of thine therefore that either immediately or afar off, hath not reference to the
common good, that is an exorbitant, and disorderly action; yea it is seditious; as one among
the people who from such and such a consent
and unity, should factiously divide and separate
himself.

M. A. ix. 21.

T HERE is but one light of the sun, though it
be intercepted by walls and mountains, and
other thousand objects. There is but one common
soul, though divided into innumerable particular
essences and natures.

M A. xii. 23.

96

TO judge of reasonable and unreasonable, we make use not only of a due estimation of things without us, but of what relates to each person's particular character. Thus, it is reasonable for one man to submit to a dirty disgraceful office, who considers this only, that if he does not submit to it he shall be whipped, and lose his dinner; but if he does, that he has nothing hard or disagreeable to suffer: whereas to another it appears insupportable, not only to submit to such an office himself, but to bear with anyone else who does. If you ask me, then, whether you shall do this dirty office or not, I will tell you, it is a more valuable thing to get a dinner, than not; and a greater disgrace to be whipped than not to be whipped: so that, if you measure yourself by these things, go and do your office.

"Ay, but this is not suitable to my character."

It is you who are to consider that, not I: for it is you who know yourself, what value you set upon yourself, and at what rate you sell yourself. for different people sell themselves at different prices.

E. D. i. 2, 2.

" AND why did he speak?" You may as well
ask, Why was he Apollo, why doth he
deliver oracles, why hath he placed himself in
such a post as a prophet and the fountain of truth,
to whom the inhabitants of the world should re-
sort? Why is Know Thyself inscribed on the
front of his temple, when no one minds it?

Did Socrates prevail on all who came to him, to
take care of themselves? Not on the thousandth
part; but however, being, as he himself declares,
divinely appointed to such a post, he never de-
serted it. What doth he say even to the judges?
"If you would acquit me, on condition that I
should no longer act as I do now, I will not accept
it, nor desist, but I will accost all I meet, whether
young or old, and interrogate them just in the same
manner, but particularly you, my fellow-citizens, as
you are more nearly related to me." "Are you so
curious and officious, Socrates? What is it to you
how we act?"—"What do you say? While you
are of the same community, and the same kindred
with me, shall you be careless of yourself, and
show yourself a bad citizen to the city, a bad
kinsman to your kindred, and a bad neighbour
to your neighbourhood?"

E. D. iii. 1, 3, 4

OBSERVE yourselves in your actions, and you will find of what sect you are. You will find that most of you are Epicureans, a few Peripatetics, and those but loose ones. For, by what action will you prove that you think virtue equal, and even superior, to all other things? Show me a Stoic if you have one. Where? Or how should you? You can show, indeed, a thousand who repeat the Stoic reasonings. But do they repeat the Epicurean worse! Are they not just as perfect in the Peripatetic? Who, then, is a Stoic? As we call that a Phidian statue, which is formed according to the art of Phidias, so show me some one person, formed according to the principles which he professes

E. D. ii. 19, 3.

SHOW me one who is sick, and happy; in danger, and happy; dying, and happy; exiled, and happy; disgraced, and happy. Show him me, for, by heaven, I long to see a Stoic. But (you will say) you have not one perfectly formed. Show me, then, one who is forming, one who is approaching towards this character. Do me this favour. Do not refuse an old man a sight which he hath never yet seen. Let any of you show me a human soul, willing to have the same sentiments with those of God, not to accuse either God or man, not to be disappointed of its desire, or incur its aversion, not to be angry, not to be envious, not to be jealous, in a word, willing from a man to become a God, and, in this poor mortal body, aiming to have fellowship with Jupiter. Show him to me. But you cannot. Why, then, do you impose upon yourselves, and play tricks with others?

E. D. ii. 19, 3.

A CYNIC must besides have so much patience as to seem insensible and a stone to the vulgar. No one reviles, no one beats, no one affronts him; but he hath surrendered his body to be treated at pleasure by anyone who will. For he remembers that the inferior, in whatever instance it is the inferior, must be conquered by the superior, and the body is inferior to the multitude, the weaker to the stronger. He never therefore enters into a combat where he can be conquered, but immediately gives up what belongs to others; he doth not claim what is slavish and dependent; but, where choice and the use of the Appearances are concerned, you will see that he hath so many eyes, you would say Argos was blind to him. Is his assent ever precipitate? His pursuits ever rash? His desire ever disappointed? His aversion ever incurred? His intention ever fruitless? Is he ever querulous, ever dejected, ever envious? Here lies all his attention and application. With regard to other things, he snores supine. All is peace. There is no robber, no tyrant of the choice.

E. D. iii. 22, 14.

BUT above all, the ruling faculty of a Cynic must be purer than the sun, otherwise he must necessarily be a common cheat, and a rascal, if, while he is guilty of some vice himself, he reproves others. For, consider how the case stands. Arms and guards give a power to common kings and tyrants of reproving and of punishing delinquents, though they are wicked themselves; but to a Cynic, instead of arms and guards, conscience gives this power, when he knows that he hath watched and laboured for mankind; that he hath slept pure, and waked still purer; and that he hath regulated all his thoughts as the friend, as the minister of the gods, as a partner of the empire of Jupiter; that he is ready to say upon all occasions,

Conduct me, Jove; and thou, O Destiny.

And, "If it thus pleases the gods, thus let it be." Why should he not dare to speak boldly to his own brethren, to his children; in a word, to his kindred?

E. D. iii. 22, 13.

HENCE he who is thus qualified is neither impertinent nor a busybody, for he is not busied about the affairs of others, but his own, when he oversees the transactions of men. Otherwise say that a general is a busybody when he oversees, examines, and watches his soldiers, and punishes the disorderly. But if you reprove others at the very time that you have a cake under your own arm, I will ask you: Had you not better, sir, go into a corner and eat up what you have stolen? But what have you to do with the concerns of others? For what are you? Are you the bull in the herd, or the queen of the bees? Show me such ensigns of empire as she hath from nature. But, if you are a drone, and arrogate to yourself the kingdom of the bees, do not you think that your fellow-citizens will drive you out, just as the bees do the drones?

E. D. iii. 22, 13.

Un   ·®

IF anyone comes and tells you, that in a dispute which was the best of the philosophers, one of the company said that such a one was the only philosopher, that little soul of yours grows to the size of two cubits, instead of an inch ; but if another should come and say, "You are mistaken, he is not worth hearing, for what doth he know? He hath the first rudiments, but nothing more," you are thunderstruck ; you presently turn pale and cry out, "I will show him what a man, and how great a philosopher, I am." It is evident what you are by these very things ; why do you aim to show it by others? Do not you know that Diogenes showed some sophist in this manner by extending his middle finger; and, when he was mad with rage, This, says Diogenes, is he ; I have showed him to you. For a man is not shown in the same sense as a stone, or a piece of wood, by the finger ; but whoever shows his principles, shows him as a man.

E. D. iii. 2, 4.

FROM an unseasonable regard to divination, we omit many duties. For what can the diviner see, besides death, or danger, or sickness, or, in short, things of this kind? When it is necessary, then, to expose oneself to danger for a friend, or even a duty to die for him, what occasion have I for divination? Have not I a diviner within, who hath told me the essence of good and evil, and who explains to me the indications of both? What further need, then, have I of the entrails of victims, or the flight of birds!

E. D. ii. 7, 1.

WHAT use is there of suspicion at all? or, why should thoughts of mistrust, and suspicion concerning that which is future, trouble thy mind at all? What now is to be done, if thou mayest search and inquire into that, what needs thou care for more? And if thou art well able to perceive it alone, let no man divert thee from it. But if alone thou dost not so well perceive it, suspend thine action, and take advice from the best. And if there be anything else that doth hinder thee, go on with prudence and discretion, according to the present occasion and opportunity, still proposing that unto thyself, which thou dost conceive most right and just. For to hit that aright, and to speed in the prosecution of it, must needs be happiness, since it is that only which we can truly and properly be said to miss of, or, miscarry in.

M. A. x. 13.

A S a traveller inquires the road of the person he meets, without any desire for that which turns to the right hand, more than to the left; for he wishes for neither of these, but that only which leads him properly. Thus we should come to God as to a guide. Just as we make use of our eyes, not persuading them to show us one object rather than another, but receiving such as they present to us. But now we hold the bird with fear and trembling, and, in our invocations to God, entreat Him, "Lord, have mercy upon me: suffer me to come off safe." You wretch! would you have anything, then, but what is best? And what is best, but what pleases God? Why do you, as far as in you lies, corrupt your judge and seduce your adviser?

E. D. II. 7, 3.

G OD now brings me hither, now sends me thither; shows me to mankind, poor, without authority, sick; sends me to Gyaros, leads me to prison: not that He hates me; heaven forbid! For who hates the best of his servants? Nor that He neglects me, for He doth not neglect any one of the smallest things; but to exercise me, and make use of me as a witness to others. Appointed to such a service, do I still care where I am, or with whom, or what is said of me, instead of being wholly attentive to God, and to His orders and commands?

E. D. iii. 24, 6.

A WISE and good man, mindful who he is and whence he came, and by whom he was produced, is attentive only how he may fill his post regularly and dutifully to God. "Is it thy pleasure I should any longer continue in being? I will continue free, spirited, agreeably to thy pleasure; for thou hast made me incapable of restraint in what is my own. But thou hast no further use for me? Fare thou well! I have stayed thus long for thy sake alone, and no other, and now I depart in obedience to thee."—"How do you depart?" —"Again, agreeably to thy pleasure; as free, as thy servant, as one sensible of thy commands and thy prohibitions. But while I am employed in thy service, what wouldst thou have me be? A prince or a private man, a senator or a plebeian, a soldier or a general, a preceptor or the master of a family? Whatever post or rank thou shalt assign me, like Socrates, I will die a thousand times rather than desert it. Where wouldst thou have me be? At Rome or at Athens, at Thebes or at Gyaros? Only remember me there. If thou shalt send me where men cannot live conformably to nature, I do not depart from thence in disobedience to thy will, but as receiving my signal of retreat from thee. I do not desert thee; heaven forbid! but I perceive thou hast no use for me. If a life conformable to nature be granted, I will seek no other place but that in which I am, nor any other company but those with whom I am."

E. D. iii. 24, 5.

BE not surprised, if other animals have all things necessary to the body ready provided for them, not only meat and drink but lodging : that they want neither shoes, nor bedding, nor clothes, while we stand in need of all these. For they not being made for themselves, but for service, it was not fit that they should be formed so as to need the help of others. For, consider what it would be for us to take care, not only for ourselves, but for sheep and asses too, how they should be clothed, how shod, and how they should eat and drink. But as soldiers are ready for their commander, shod, clothed, and armed (for it would be a grievous thing for a colonel to be obliged to go through his regiment to put on their shoes and clothes), so nature likewise has formed the animals made for service, ready provided, and standing in need of no further care. Thus one little boy, with only a crook, drives a flock.

But now we, instead of being thankful for this, complain of God that there is not the same kind of care taken of us likewise. And yet, good heaven ! any one thing in the creation is sufficient to demonstrate a providence to a modest and grateful mind. Not to instance at present in great things, but only in the very production of milk from grass, cheese from milk, and wool from skins : who formed and contrived these things ? No one, say you. O surprising stupidity, and want of shame !

E. D. i. 16, 1, 2.

"PRAY, sir, can you tell me to whom you entrust your horses?"—"Yes, certainly." "Is it, then, to anyone indifferently, though he be ignorant of horsemanship?"—"By no means." "To whom do you entrust your gold, or your silver, or your clothes?"—"Not to anyone indifferently." "And did you ever consider to whom you committed the care of your body?"—"Yes, surely." "To one skilled in exercise, or medicine, I suppose?"—"Without doubt." "Are these things your chief good; or are you possessed of something better than all of them?"—"What do you mean?" "Something which makes use of these, and proves and deliberates about each of them?"—"What then, do you mean the soul?" "You have guessed right; for indeed I do mean that."—"I do really think it a much better possession than all the rest."

E. D. ii. 12, 1.

Un   ®

"CAN you show us, then, in what manner you have taken care of this soul? For it is not probable that a person of your wisdom, and approved character in the State, should carelessly suffer the most excellent thing that belongs to you to be neglected and lost." — "No, certainly." "But do you take care of it yourself? And is it by the instructions of another, or by your own discovery how it ought to be done?" Here now comes the danger, that he may first say, Pray, good sir, what business is that of yours? What are you to me? Then, if you persist to trouble him, he may lift up his hand and give you a box on the ear. I myself was once a great admirer of this method of instruction, till I fell into such kind of adventures.

E. D. ii. 12, 1.

YOU carry a god about with you, wretch. I know nothing of it. Do you suppose I mean some god without you, of gold or silver? It is within yourself you wrong him, and profane him, without being sensible of it, by impure thoughts and unclean actions.

E. D. ii. 8, 2.

HAVE you not God? Do you seek any other, while you have Him? Or will He tell you any other than these things? If you were a statue of Phidias, either Zeus or Athena, you would remember both yourself and the artist; and, if you had any sense, you would endeavour to do nothing unworthy of him who formed you, or of yourself: nor to appear in an unbecoming manner to spectators. And are you now careless how you appear, because you are the workmanship of Jupiter?

E. D. ii. 8, 3.

AND yet, what comparison is there, either between the artists or the things they have formed? What work of any artist contains in itself those faculties which are shown in forming it? Is it anything but marble, or brass, or gold, or ivory? And the Athena of Phidias, when its hand is once extended and a Victory placed in it, remains in that attitude for ever. But the works of God are endued with motion, breath, the use of the appearances of things, judgment. Being, then, the formation of such an artist, will you dishonour him, especially when he hath not only formed, but entrusted and given the guardianship of you to yourself? Will you not only be forgetful of this, but, moreover, dishonour the trust? If God had committed some orphan to your charge, would you have been thus careless of him? He hath delivered yourself to your care, and says, " I had no one fitter to be trusted than you . preserve this person for me, such as he is by nature; modest, faithful, sublime, unterrified, dispassionate, tranquil." And will you not preserve him?

E D. ii 8, 3.

I COME therefore to the diviner and interpreter of these things, and say, "Inspect the entrails for me : what is signified to me?" Having taken and laid them open, he thus interprets them :— You have a choice, man, incapable of being restrained or compelled. This is written here in the entrails I will show you this first in the faculty of assent. Can any one restrain you from assenting to truth?—"No one"—Can anyone compel you to admit a falsehood?—"No one."—You see, then, that you have in this topic a choice incapable of being restrained or compelled or hindered. Well, is it any otherwise with regard to pursuit and desire? What can conquer one pursuit?— "Another pursuit."—What desire and aversion?— "Another desire and another aversion." If you set death before me (say you) you compel me No; not what is set before you doth it, but your principle, that it is better to do such or such a thing than to die. Here, again, you see it is your own principle which compels you—that is, choice compels choice. For, if God had constituted that portion which He hath separated from His own offence and given to us, capable of being restrained or compelled, either by Himself or by any other, He would not have been God, nor have taken care of us in a due manner

E. D. i. 17, 2.

Un   ®

OUR life is a warfare, and a mere pilgrimage.

M. A. ii. 15.

THOU hast taken ship, thou hast sailed, thou
art come to land : go out, if to another life,
there also shalt thou find gods, who are everywhere. If all life and sense shall cease, then
shalt thou cease also to be subject to either
pains, or pleasures.

M. A. iii. 4.

THE art of true living in this world, is more
like a wrestler's than a dancer's practice. For
in this they both agree, to teach a man, whatsoever
falls upon him, that he may be ready for it, and
that nothing may cast him down.

M. A. vii. 33.

IS anyone preferred before you at an entertainment, or in a compliment, or in being admitted to a consultation? If these things are good, you ought to rejoice that he hath got them; and if they are evil, do not be grieved that you have not got them. And remember that you cannot, without using the same means to acquire things not in our own power, expect to be thought worthy of an equal share of them. For how can he who doth not frequent the door of any man, doth not attend him, doth not praise him, have an equal share with him who doth? You are unjust, then, and insatiable, if you are unwilling to pay the price for which these things are sold, and would have them for nothing.

E. M. 25.

FOR how much are lettuces sold? A halfpenny, for instance. If another, then, paying
a halfpenny, takes the lettuces, and you, not paying it, go without them, do not imagine that he
hath gained any advantage over you. For as he
hath the lettuces, so you have the halfpenny which
you did not give. So, in the present case, you
have not been invited to such a person's entertainment, because you have not paid him the
price for which a supper is sold. It is sold for
praise ; it is sold for attendance Give him then
the value, if it be for your advantage. But if you
would, at the same time, not pay the one and yet
receive the other, you are insatiable, and a blockhead. Have you nothing, then, instead of the
supper? Yes, indeed, you have : the not praising
him, whom you do not like to praise; the not
bearing with his behaviour at coming in.

E. M. 25

WHEN we are invited to an entertainment, we take what we find; and if anyone should bid the master of the house set fish or tarts before him, he would be thought absurd. Yet, in the world, we ask the gods for what they do not give us, and that though they have given us so many things.

E. FR. 12.

IN every feast remember that there are two guests to be entertained, the body and the soul, and that what you give the body you presently lose, but what you give the soul remains for ever

E. FR. 27.

AGRIPPINUS, when Florus was considering whether he should go to Nero's shows, so as to perform some part in them himself, bid him go. —"But why do not you go then?" says Florus. "Because," replied Agrippinus, "I do not deliberate about it." For he who once sets himself about such considerations, and goes to calculating the worth of external things, approaches very near to those who forget their own character.

E. D. i. 2, 3.

.

IT would be best if, both while you are person-
ally making your preparations, and while you
are feasting at table, you could give among the
servants part of what is before you.   But, if such
a thing be difficult at that time, remember that
you, who are not weary, are attended by those
who are, you, who are eating and drinking, by
those who are not; you, who are talking, by
those who are silent; you, who are at ease, by
those who are under constraint; and thus you will
never be heated into any unreasonable passion
yourself, nor do any mischief by provoking another.

E. FR. 30.

WHEN a person inquired, how any one might eat acceptably to the gods: If he eats with justice, says Epictetus, and gratitude, and fairly and temperately and decently, must he not also eat acceptably to the gods? And when you call for hot water, and your servant doth not hear you, or, if he doth, brings it only warm; or perhaps is not to be found at home; then not to be angry, or burst with passion, is not this acceptable to the gods?

E. D. 1. 13, 1.

IN the mind that is once truly disciplined and purged, thou canst not find anything, either foul or impure, or as it were festered: nothing that is either servile, or affected: no partial tie; no malicious averseness; nothing obnoxious; nothing concealed. The life of such an one, Death can never surprise as imperfect; as of an Actor, that should die before he had ended, or the play itself were at an end, a man might speak.

M. A. iii. 9

MAY I

IN parties of conversation, avoid a frequent and excessive mention of your own actions and dangers. For, however agreeable it may be to yourself to mention the risks you have run, it is not equally agreeable to others to hear your adventures. Avoid, likewise, an endeavour to excite laughter. For this is a slippery point, which may throw you into vulgar manners, and, besides, may be apt to lessen you in the esteem of your acquaintance. Approaches to indecent discourse are likewise dangerous. Whenever, therefore, anything of this sort happens, if there be a proper opportunity, rebuke him who makes advances that way; or, at least, by silence and blushing and a forbidding look, show yourself to be displeased by such talk.

E. M. 33.

I MAY be at a loss, perhaps, to give a reason how sensation is performed, whether it be diffused universally, or reside in a particular part; for I find difficulties that shock me in each case; but, that you and I are not the same person, I very exactly know.

How so?

Why, I never, when I have a mind to swallow anything, carry it to your mouth, but my own. I never, when I wanted to take a loaf, took a brush; but went directly to the loaf, as fit to answer my purpose. And do you yourselves, who deny all evidence of the senses, act any otherwise? Who of you, when he intended to go into a bath, ever went into a mill?

E. D. i. 27, 2.

WHAT are you doing, man? You contradict yourself every day, and yet you will not give up these paltry cavils. When you eat, where do you carry your hand? To your mouth, or to your eye? When you bathe, where do you go? Do you ever call a kettle a dish; or a spoon a spit? If I were a servant to one of these gentlemen, were it at the hazard of being flayed every day, I would plague him. "Throw some oil into the bath, boy." I would take pickle and pour upon his head. "What is this?" Really, sir, an appearance struck me so perfectly alike, as not to be distinguished from oil. "Give me the soup." I would carry him a dish full of vinegar. "Did not I ask for the soup?" Yes, sir, this is the soup. "Is not this vinegar?" Why so, more than soup? "Take it and smell to it; take it and taste it." How do you know, then, but our senses deceive us? If I had three or four fellow-servants to join with me, I would make him either choke with passion and burst, or change his opinions. But now they insult us by making use of the gifts of nature, while in words they destroy them. Grateful and modest men, truly!

E. D. ii. 20, 6.

MY friend Heraclitus, in a trifling suit about a little estate at Rhodes, after having proved to the judges that his cause was good, when he came to the conclusion of his speech, "I will not entreat you," says he, "nor care what judgment you give : for it is rather you who are to be judged than I." And thus he lost his suit. What need was there of this? Be content not to entreat : do not tell them, too, that you will not entreat, unless it be a proper time to provoke the judges designedly, as in the case of Socrates. But if you too are preparing such a speech, what do you wait for? Why do you submit to be tried? For if you wish to be hanged, have patience, and the gibbet will come. But if you choose rather to submit, and make your defence as well as you can, all the rest is to be ordered accordingly· with a due regard, however, to the preservation of your own character.

E D. ii. 2, 3.

WHEN children come to us clapping their hands and saying: "To-morrow is the good feast of Saturn," do we tell them that good doth not consist in such things? By no means: but we clap our hands along with them. Thus, when you are unable to convince anyone, consider him as a child, and clap your hands with him; or if you will not do that, at least hold your tongue

E. D. i. 29, 5.

I ONCE saw a person weeping and embracing the knees of Epaphroditus, and deploring his hard fortune that he had not £50,000 left. What said Epaphroditus, then? Did he laugh at him, as we should do? No; but cried out with astonishment: "Poor man! How could you be silent? How could you bear it?"

E. D. 1. 26, 2.

ONLY give any of us that you please some illiterate person for an antagonist, and he will not find out how to treat him. But when he hath a little moved the man, if he happens to answer beside the purpose, he knows not how to deal with him any further; but either reviles or laughs at him, and says, "He is an illiterate fellow; there is no making anything of him." Yet a guide, when he perceives his charge going out of the way, doth not revile and ridicule and then leave him; but leads him into the right path. Do you also show your antagonist the truth, and you will see that he will follow. But till you do show it, do not ridicule him; but rather be sensible of your own incapacity.

E. D. ii. 12, 1.

WILL this querulousness, this murmuring, this complaining and dissembling never be at an end? What, then, is it that troubleth thee? Doth any new thing happen unto thee? What dost thou so wonder at? At the cause, or the matter? Behold either by itself, is either of that weight and moment indeed? And besides these, there is not anything. But thy duty towards the 'gods also, it is time that thou shouldst acquit thyself of it with more goodness and simplicity.

M. A. ix. 35.

MANY of those things that trouble and straighten thee, it is in thy power to cut off, as wholly depending from mere conceit and opinion, and then thou shalt have room enough.

M. A. ix. 3.

USE thyself even unto those things that thou dost at first despair of For the left hand we see, which for the most part lieth idle because not used, yet doth it hold the bridle with more strength than the right, because it hath been used unto it.

M. A. xii. 5.

REMEMBER that you are an actor in a drama, of such a kind as the author pleases to make it. If short, of a short one; if long, of a long one. If it be his pleasure you should act a poor man, a cripple, a governor, or a private person, see that you act it naturally. For this is your business, to act well the character assigned you; to choose it, is another's.

E. M. 17.

WHAT, then, would anybody have you dress yourself out to the utmost? By no means, except in those things where our nature requires it; in reason, principles, actions; but, in our persons, only as far as neatness, as far as not to give offence. But if you hear that it is not right to wear purple, you must go, I suppose, and roll your cloak in the mud, or tear it.—"But where should I have a fine cloak?"—You have water, man; wash it. "What an amiable youth is here! How worthy this old man to love and be loved!" —A fit person to be trusted with the instruction of our sons and daughters, and attended by young people, as occasion may require—to read them lectures on a dunghill! Every deviation proceeds from something human, but this approaches very nearly towards being not human.

E. D. iv. 11, 5.

DO you think you deserve to have an unpleasant odour? Be it so. But do those deserve to suffer by it who sit near you, who are placed at table with you, who salute you? Either go into a desert, as you deserve, or live solitary at home, and smell yourself; for it is fit you should enjoy your nastiness alone. But to what sort of character doth it belong to live in a city, and behave so carelessly and inconsiderately? If nature had trusted even a horse to your care, would you have overlooked and neglected him? Now, consider your body as committed to you instead of a horse. Wash it, rub it, take care that it may not be anyone's aversion, nor disgust anyone. Who is not more disgusted at a stinking, unwholesome-looking sloven, than at a person who hath been rolled in filth? The stench of the one is adventitious from without, but that which arises from want of care is a kind of inward putrefaction.

E. D. iv. 11, 3.

DO not say to what excels, Who are you? If you do, it will, somehow or other, find a voice to tell you, "I am like the purple thread in a garment. Do not expect me to be like the rest, or find fault with my nature, which hath distinguished me from others."

What then, am I such a one? How should I? Indeed, are you such a one as to be able to hear the truth? I wish you were. But, however, since I am condemned to wear a grey beard and a cloak, and you come to me as to a philosopher, I will not treat you cruelly, nor as if I despaired of you, but will ask you—Whom is it, young man, whom you would render beautiful? Know first who you are, and then adorn yourself accordingly. You are a man ; that is, a mortal animal, capable of a rational use of the appearances of things. And what is this rational use? A perfect conformity to nature. What have you then particularly excellent? Is it the animal part? No. The mortal? No. That which is capable of the use of the appearances of things? No. The excellence lies in the rational part. Adorn and beautify this, but leave your hair to him who formed it, as he thought good.

E. D. iii. 1, 4, 5.

IF you would have your house securely inhabited, imitate the Spartan Lycurgus. And as he did not enclose his city with walls, but fortified the inhabitants with virtue, and preserved the city always free, so you do likewise; not surround yourself with a great courtyard, nor raise high towers, but strengthen those that live with you by benevolence and fidelity and friendship. And thus nothing hurtful will enter, even if the whole band of wickedness was set in array against it.

E. FR. 40.

THERE is nothing more shameful than perfidious friendship.

M. A. xi. 7.

HE is the master of every other person who is able to confer or remove whatever that person wishes to have or to avoid. Whoever then would be free, let him wish nothing, let him decline nothing, which depends on others, else he must necessarily be a slave.

E. M. 14.

133

Un   ®

REMEMBER that you must behave in life as at an entertainment. Is anything brought round to you? Put out your hand and take your share with moderation. Doth it pass by you? Do not stop it. Is it not yet come? Do not stretch forth your desire towards it, but wait till it reaches you.

E. M. 15.

LET death and exile, and all other things which appear terrible, be daily before your eyes, but chiefly death, and you will never entertain any abject thought, nor too eagerly covet anything.

E. M. 21.

AT a feast, to choose the largest share is very suitable to the bodily appetite, but utterly inconsistent with the social spirit of an entertainment. When you eat with another, then, remember not only the value of those things which are set before you to the body, but the value of that behaviour which ought to be observed towards the person who gives the entertainment.

E. M. 36

WHO is it that hath fitted the sword to the scabbard, and the scabbard to the sword? Is it no one? From the very construction of a complete work, we are used to declare positively, that it must be the operation of some artificer, and not the effect of mere chance. Doth every such work, then, demonstrate an artificer; and do not visible objects, and the sense of seeing, and Light, demonstrate one?

E. D. i. 6, 2.

SEE the practice of those who play skilfully at ball. No one contends for the ball, as either a good or an evil; but how he may throw and catch it again. Here lies the address, here the art, the nimbleness, the sagacity; that I may not be able to catch it, even if I hold up my lap for it; another may catch it whenever I throw it. But if we catch or throw it with fear or perturbation, what kind of play will this be? How shall we keep ourselves steady, or how see the order of the game? One will say, Throw; another, Do not throw; a third, You have thrown once already This is a mere quarrel, not a play.

E D ii 5, 3.

I S freedom anything else than the power of living
as we like?

Nothing else.

Well tell me, then, do you like to live in error?
We do not. No one, sure, that lives in error
is free.

Do you like to live in fear? Do you like to live
in sorrow? Do you like to live in perturbation?

By no means.

No one, therefore, in a state of fear, or sorrow,
or perturbation, is free; but whoever is delivered
from sorrow, fear, and perturbation, by the same
means is delivered likewise from slavery.

E. D. ii. 1, 4

I WOULD be the purple, that small and shining thing, which gives a lustre and beauty to the rest.

E. D. i. 2, 3.

FOR as for him who is the Administrator of all, he will make good use of thee whether thou wilt or no, and make thee (as a part and member of the whole) so to co-operate with him, that whatsoever thou doest, shall turn to the furtherance of his own counsels, and resolutions. But be not thou for shame such a part of the whole, as that vile and ridiculous verse (which Chrysippus in a place doth mention) is a part of the Comedy.

M. A. vi. 37.

PAY in, before you are called upon, what is due to the public, and you will never be asked for what is not due.

E. FR. 72.

PRISCUS HELVIDIUS, when Vespasian had sent to forbid his going to the senate, answered, "It is in your power to prevent my continuing a senator; but while I am one, I must go." —"Well then, at least be silent there."—"Do not ask my opinion, and I will be silent."—"But I must ask it."—"And I must speak what appears to me to be right."—"But if you do, I will put you to death."—"Did I ever tell you that I was immortal? You will do your part, and I mine: It is yours to kill, and mine to die intrepid; yours to banish me, mine to depart untroubled."

What good, then, did Priscus do, who was but a single person? Why what good does the purple do to the garment? What but the being a shining character in himself, and setting a good example to others? Another, perhaps, if in such circumstances Cæsar had forbidden his going to the senate, would have answered, "I am obliged to you for excusing me." But such a one he would not have forbidden to go, well knowing that he would either sit like a statue, or, if he spoke, he would say what he knew to be agreeable to Cæsar, and would overdo it by adding still more.

E. D. i. 2, 4, 5.

DIOGENES used to say, "Ever since Antisthenes made me free, I have ceased to be a
slave" How did he make him free? Hear what
he says. "He taught. me what was my own, and
what not. An estate is not my own. Kindred,
domestics, friends, reputation, familiar places,
manner of life, all belong to another." "What is
your own, then?" "The use of the appearances
of things. He showed me that I have this, not
subject to restraint or compulsion; no one can
hinder or force me to use them any otherwise than
I please. Who, then, after this, hath any power
over me? Philip, or Alexander, or Perdiccas, or
the Persian king? Whence should they have it?
For he that is to be subdued by man must, long
before, be subdued by things. He, therefore, of
whom neither pleasure nor pain, nor fame nor
riches, can get the better, and who is able, whenever he thinks fit, to throw away his whole body
with contempt, and depart, whose slave can he
ever be?"

E. D. iii. 23, 4.

WE will allow those creatures only to be free who do not endure captivity; but, as soon as they are taken, die, and escape. Thus Diogenes somewhere says, that the only way to freedom is to die with ease. And he writes to the Persian king, "You can no more enslave the Athenians than you can fish."—"How? What, shall not I take them?"—"If you do take them," says he, "they will leave you, and be gone like fish. For take a fish, and it dies. And, if the Athenians too die as soon as you have taken them, of what use are your warlike preparations?" This is the voice of a free man, who had examined the matter in earnest, and, as it might be expected, found it out. But, if you seek it where it is not, what wonder if you never find it?

E. D. iv. 1, 6.

CEASE to make yourselves slaves, first of
things, and then upon their account, of the
men who have the power either to bestow or take
them away. Is there any advantage then to be
gained from these men? From all, even from a
reviler. What advantage doth a wrestler gain
from him with whom he exercises himself, before
the combat? The greatest. Why, just in the
same manner I exercise myself with this man.
He exercises me in patience, in gentleness, in
meekness. Is my neighbour a bad one? He is
so to himself; but a good one to me. He exercises my good temper, my moderation. Is my
father bad? To himself, but not to me. "This
is the rod of Hermes. Touch with it whatever
you please, and it will become gold." No; but
bring whatever you please, and I will turn it into
good. Bring sickness, death, want, reproach,
capital trial. All these, by the rod of Hermes,
shall turn to advantage.

E. D. iii. 20, 1.

Un   ®

FREEDOM is the name of virtue ; and slavery, of vice

E. F. 7.

NO one is free, who doth not command himself.

E. F. 109.

WHAT is wickedness? It is that which many times and often thou hast already seen and known in the world. And so oft as anything doth happen that might otherwise trouble thee, let this memento presently come to thy mind, that it is that which thou hast already often seen and known. Generally, above and below, thou shalt find but the same things. The very same things whereof ancient stories, middle-age stories, and fresh stories are full : whereof towns are full, and houses full. There is nothing that is new. All things that are, are both usual and of little continuance.

M. A. ii. 1.

THE man who is unrestrained, who hath all things in his power as he wills, is free; but he who may be restrained, or compelled, or hindered, or thrown into any condition against his will, is a slave. "And who is unrestrained?"— He that desires none of those things that belong to others. "And what are those things which belong to others?"—Those which are not in our own power, either to have or not to have.

E. D. iv. 1, 14.

THE things themselves (which either to get or to avoid thou art put to so much trouble) come not unto thee themselves; but thou in a manner goest unto them. Let then thine own judgment and opinion concerning those things be at rest; and as for the things themselves, they stand still and quiet, without any noise or stir at all; and so shall all pursuing and flying cease.

M. A. xi. 10.

H E is free who lives as he likes; who is not subject either to compulsion, to restraint, or to violence; whose pursuits are unhindered, his desires successful, his aversions unincurred. Who, then, would wish to lead a wrong course of life? —"No one." Who would live deceived, prone to mistake, unjust, dissolute, discontented, dejected? —"No one." No wicked man, then, lives as he likes; therefore neither is he free. And who would live in sorrow, fear, envy, pity; with disappointed desires, and incurred aversions?—"No one." Do we then find any of the wicked exempt from sorrow, fear, disappointed desires, incurred aversions?—"Not one." Consequently, then, not free.

E. D. iv. 1, 1.

STUDY these points, these principles, these discourses, contemplate these examples, if you would be free, if you desire the thing in proportion to its value. And where is the wonder that you should purchase so great a thing at the price of others, so many, and so great? Some hang themselves, others break their necks, and sometimes even whole cities have been destroyed, for that which is reputed freedom; and will not you, for the sake of the true and secure and inviolable freedom, repay God what He hath given when He demands it? Will you not study, not only as Plato says, to die, but to be tortured and banished and scourged, and, in short, to give up all that belongs to others? If not, you will be a slave among slaves, though you were ten thousand times a consul; and, even though you should rise to the palace, you will be nevertheless so. And you will feel that though philosophers (as Cleanthes says) do, perhaps, talk contrary to common opinion, yet not contrary to reason. For you will find it true, in fact, that the things that are eagerly followed and admired are of no use to those who have gained them; while they who have not yet gained them imagine that, if they are acquired, every good will come along with them; and then, when they are acquired, there is the same feverishness, the same agitation, the same nauseating, and the same desire of what is absent.

E. D. iv. 1, 19.

BUT the tyrant will chain—what?—A leg.—He will take away—what?—A head.—What is there, then, that he can neither chain nor take away?—The will and choice. Hence the advice of the ancients—Know thyself.

E. D. i. 18, 2.

SUPPOSE that at the Palæstra somebody hath all torn thee with his nails, and hath broken thy head. Well, thou art wounded. Yet thou dost not exclaim; thou art not offended with him. Thou dost not suspect him for it afterwards, as one that watched to do thee a mischief. Yea, even then, though thou doest thy best to save thyself from him, yet not from him as an enemy. It is not by way of any suspicious indignation, but by way of gentle and friendly declination. Keep the same mind and disposition in other parts of thy life also. For many things there be, which we must conceive and apprehend, as though we had had to do with an antagonist at the Palæstra. For as I said, it is very possible for us to avoid and decline, though we neither suspect, nor hate.

M. A. vi. 19.

146

WHAT, then¹ do you philosophers teach us a contempt of kings?

By no means. Who of us teaches anyone to contend with them about things of which they have the command? Take my body, take my possessions, take my reputation, take those who are about me. If I persuade anyone to contend for these things in his own, accuse me with justice.—"Ay, but I would command your principles too."—And who hath given you that power? How can you conquer the principle of another?— By applying terror I will conquer it.—Do not you see that what conquers itself is not conquered by another? And nothing but itself can conquer the choice. Hence, too, the most excellent and equitable love of God, that the better should always prove superior to the worse.

E. D. i. 29, 2.

GOD says, "If you wish for good, receive it from yourself." You say, No; but from another. —"Nay; but from yourself." In consequence of this, when a tyrant threatens and sends for me; I say, Against what is your threatening pointed? If he says, "I will chain you"; I answer, It is my hands and feet that you threaten. If he says, "I will cut off your head"; I answer, It is my head that you threaten. If he says, "I will throw you into prison"; I answer, It is the whole of this paltry body that you threaten : and, if he threatens banishment, just the same.

Doth not he threaten you, then?

If I am persuaded that these things are nothing to me, he doth not; but, if I fear any of them, it is me that he threatens Whom, after all, is it that I fear? The master of what? Of things in my own power? Of these no one is the master. Of things not in my power? And what are these to me?

E. D i. 29, 1.

THEY kill me, they cut my flesh: they perse-
cute my person with curses. What then?
May not thy mind for all this continue pure,
prudent, temperate, just? As a fountain of sweet
and clear water, though she be cursed by some
stander by, yet do her springs nevertheless still
run as sweet and clear as before; yea though
either dirt or dung be thrown in, yet is it no
sooner thrown, than dispersed, and she cleared.
She cannot be dyed or, infected by it. What
then must I do, that I may have within myself
an overflowing fountain, and not a well? Beget
thyself by continual pains and endeavours to true
liberty with charity, and true simplicity and
modesty.

M. A. viii. 50.

Un ®

A S one that tosseth up a ball. And what is a
ball the better, if the motion of it be upwards;
or the worse if it be downwards; or if it chance
to fall upon the ground? So for the bubble; if
it continue, what is it the better? And if it dis-
solve, what is it the worse? And so is it of a
candle too. And so must thou reason with thyself, both in matter of fame, and in matter of
death. For as for the body itself, (the subject of
death) wouldst thou know the vileness of it?
Turn it about, that thou mayest behold it the
worst sides upwards as well, as in its more ordinary
pleasant shape; how doth it look, when it is old
and withered? when sick and pained? And as for
fame. This life is short. Both he that praiseth,
and he that is praised; he that remembers, and he
that is remembered, will soon be dust and ashes.
Besides, it is but in one corner of this part of the
world that thou art praised; and yet in this corner,
thou hast not the joint praises of all men; no nor
scarce of anyone constantly. And yet the whole
earth itself, what is it but as one point, in regard
of the whole world?

M. A. viii. 19

A S for thy life, consider what it is, a wind; not one constant wind neither, but every moment of an hour let out, and sucked in again. The third, is thy ruling part; and here consider; Thou art an old man; suffer not that excellent part to be brought in subjection, and to become slavish suffer it not to be drawn up and down with unreasonable and unsociable lusts and motions, as it were with wires and nerves; suffer it not any more, either to repine at anything now present, or to fear and fly anything to come, which the Destiny hath appointed thee.

E. D. i. 16.

151

Un ®

WHAT is it to bear a fever well? Not to blame either God or man, not to be afflicted at what happens ; to expect death in a right and becoming manner, and to do what is to be done. When the physician enters, not to dread what he may say ; nor, if he should tell you that you are in a fair way to be too much rejoiced ; for what good hath he told you? When you were in health, what good did it do you? Not to be dejected when he tells you that you are very ill ; for what is it to be very ill? To be near the separation of soul and body. What harm is there in this, then? If you are not near it now, will you not be near it hereafter? What, will the world be quite overset when you die?

E. D. iii. 10.

JUNE 1

BUT what says God? "O Epictetus, if it were possible, I had made this little body and property of thine free, and not liable to hindrance. But now do not mistake : it is not thine own, but only a finer mixture of clay. Since, then, I could not give thee this, I have given thee a certain portion of myself: this faculty of exerting the powers or pursuit and avoidance, of desire and aversion ; and, in a word, the use of the appearances of things. Taking care of this point, and making what is thy own to consist in this, thou wilt never be restrained, never be hindered; thou wilt not groan, wilt not complain, wilt not flatter anyone. How then! Do all these advantages seem small to thee?" Heaven forbid! "Let them suffice thee then, and thank the gods."

E. D. 1 1, 3.

BOLDLY make a desperate push, man, as the saying is, for prosperity, for freedom, for magnanimity. Lift up your head at last, as free from slavery. Dare to look up to God and say, "Make use of me for the future as Thou wilt. I am of the same mind; I am equal with Thee I refuse nothing which seems good to Thee. Lead me whither Thou wilt. Clothe me in whatever dress Thou wilt. Is it Thy will, that I should be in a public or a private condition, dwell here or be banished, be poor or rich? Under all these circumstances I will make Thy defence to men. I will show what the nature of everything is." No. Rather sit alone in a warm place, and wait till your mamma comes to feed you.

E. D. ii. 16, 4

154

IF Hercules had sat loitering at home, what would he have been? Eurystheus, and not Hercules. Besides, by travelling through the world, how many acquaintance and how many friends had he? But none more his friend than God, for which reason he was believed to be the son of God, and was so. In obedience to Him, he went about extirpating injustice and lawless force. But you are not Hercules, nor able to extirpate the evils of others; nor even Theseus to extirpate the evils of Attica. Extirpate your own, then. Expel, instead of Procrustes and Sciron, grief, fear, desire, envy, malevolence, avarice, effeminacy, intemperance, from your mind. But these can be no otherwise expelled than by looking up to God alone as your pattern; by attaching yourself to Him alone, and being consecrated to His commands. If you wish for anything else, you will, with sighs and groans, follow what is stronger than you, always seeking prosperity without, and never able to find it. For you seek it where it is not, and neglect to seek it where it is.

E. D. ii. 16, 4

WHAT is by nature free, cannot be disturbed
or restrained by anything but itself.   But
its own principles disturb it.   Thus, when the
tyrant says to anyone: "I will chain your leg":
he who values his leg, cries out for pity: while he
who sets the value on his own will and choice,
says: "If you imagine it for your interest, chain
it." —"What! do not you care?"—No; I do not
care.—"I will show you that I am master."—You?
How should you?   God has set me free.   What!
do you think He would suffer His own son to be
enslaved?   You are master of my carcase   Take
it.—"So that when you come into my presence,
you pay no regard to me?"—No; but to myself.

E. D. i. 19, 2.

156

WHAT is our nature?
      To be free, noble-spirited, modest. (For what other animal blushes? What other hath the idea of shame?) But pleasure must be subjected to these, as an attendant and handmaid, to call forth our activity and to keep us constant in natural operations.

But I am rich and want nothing.

Then why do you pretend to philosophize? Your gold and silver plate is enough for you. What need have you of principles?

Besides, I am judge of the Greeks.

Do you know how to judge? Who hath imparted this knowledge to you?

Cæsar hath given me a commission.

Let him give you a commission to judge of music; and what good will it do you? But how were you made a judge? Whose hand have you kissed? Before whose bed-chamber have you slept? To whom have you sent presents?

But I can throw whom I please into prison.

As you may a stone.

But I can beat whom I will too.

As you may an ass. This is not a government of men.

E. D. iii. 7, 1.

DO not you know that freedom is a very beautiful and valuable thing? But for me to choose at random, and for things to happen agreeably to such a choice, may be so far from a beautiful thing as to be, of all others, the most shocking. For how do we proceed in writing? Do I choose to write the name of Dion (for instance) as I will? No; but I am taught to be willing to write it as it ought to be writ. And what is the case in music? The same. And what in every other art or science? Otherwise, it would be to no purpose to learn anything, if it was to be adapted to each one's particular humour. Is it, then, only in the greatest and principal point, that of freedom, permitted me to will at random? By no means, but true instruction is this: learning to will that things should happen as they do. And how do they happen? As the appointer of them hath appointed. He hath appointed that there should be summer and winter, plenty and dearth, virtue and vice, and all such contrarieties, for the harmony of the whole. To each of us he hath given a body and its parts, and our several properties and companions Mindful of this appointment, we should enter upon a course of education and instruction not to change the constitutions of things, which is neither put within our reach nor for our good; but that, being as they are, and as their nature is with regard to us, we may have our mind accommodated to what exists.

E. D. i. 12, 2.

WHAT makes a tyrant formidable? His guards, say you, and their swords; they who belong to the bedchamber, and they who shut out those who would go in. What is the reason, then, that, if you bring a child to him when he is surrounded by his guards, it is not afraid? Is it because the child doth not know what they mean? Suppose, then, that anyone doth know what is meant by guards, and that they are armed with swords, and, for that very reason, comes in the tyrant's way, being desirous, on account of some misfortune, to die. and seeking to die easily by the hand of another: doth such a man fear the guards? No: for he wants the very thing that renders them formidable. Well, then, if anyone without an absolute desire to live or die, but, as it may happen, comes in the way of a tyrant, what restrains his approaching him without fear? Nothing.

E. D iv. 7, 1.

WHAT, then, must I at one time be called to a trial; must another at another time be scorched by a fever; another be exposed to the sea; another die; and another be condemned?

Yes; for it is impossible, in such a body, in such a world, and among such companions, but that some or other of us must fall into such circumstances. Your business, when you come into them, is to say what you ought, to order things as you can. Then, says one, "I decide that you have acted unjustly." Much good may it do you; I have done my part. You are to look to it, whether you have done yours; for there is some danger of that too, let me tell you.

E. D. ii. 5, 5.

CONSIDER, you who are going to take your trial, what you wish to preserve, and in what to succeed. For if you wish to preserve a choice conformable to nature, you are resting safe; everything goes well, you have no trouble on your hands. While you wish to preserve what is in your own power, and which is naturally free, and are contented with that, whom have you longer to care for? For who is the master of things like these? Who can take them away? If you wish to be a man of honour and fidelity, who shall prevent you? If you wish not to be restrained or compelled, who shall compel you to desires contrary to your principles; to aversions contrary to your opinion? The judge, perhaps, will pass a sentence against you which he thinks formidable: but how can he likewise make you receive it with aversion? Since, then, desire and aversion are in your own power, what have you else to care for? Let this be your introduction, this your narration, this your proof, this your victory, this your conclusion, and this your applause.

E. D. ii. 2, 1.

BUT he who hath the power hath given sentence. "I judge you to be impious and profane." What hath befallen you?—I have been judged to be impious and profane. Anything else? — Nothing. Suppose he had passed his judgment upon an hypothetical proposition, and pronounced it to be a false conclusion, that if it be day it is light; what would have befallen the proposition? In this case who is judged; who condemned; the proposition, or he who is deceived concerning it? Doth he, who hath the power of pronouncing anything concerning you, know what pious or impious mean? Hath he made it his study, or learned it? Where? From whom? A musician would not regard him if he pronounced bass to be treble: nor a mathematician, if he passed sentence that lines drawn from the centre to the circle are not equal. And shall he, who is truly learned, regard an unlearned man, when he pronounces upon pious and impious, just and unjust?

E. D. I. 29, 7.

WHEN you are going to any one of the great, remember there is another, who sees from above what passes ; and whom you ought to please rather than man. He therefore asks you :

In the school, what did you use to call exile, and prison, and chains, and death, and defamation?

I? Indifferent things.

What, then, do you call them now? Are they at all changed ?—No.

Are you changed, then ?—No.

Tell me, then, what things are indifferent.

Things independent on choice

Tell me the consequence too.

Things independent on choice, are nothing to me.

Tell me, likewise, what appeared to us to be the good of man.

A right choice and a right use of the appearances of things,

What his end?

To follow thee.

Do you say the same things now, too?

Yes, I do say the same things, even now.

Well, go in, then, boldly, and mindful of these things: and you will see what a youth, who hath studied what he ought, is among men who have not. I protest, I imagine you will have such thoughts as these: "Why do we provide so many and great qualifications for nothing? Is the power, the antechamber, the attendants, the guards, no more than this? Is it for these that I have listened to so many dissertations? These are nothing: and I had qualified myself as for some great encounter."

E. D. i. 30.

163

Un   ®

WHENEVER you see any one subject to
another, and flattering him, contrary to
his own opinion, confidently say that he too is
not free ; and not only if he doth it for a supper,
but even if it be for a government, nay, a consulship ; but call those indeed little slaves who act
thus for the sake of little things, and the others,
as they deserve, great slaves.—" Be this, too,
agreed." Well, do you think freedom to be something independent and self-determined?—" How
can it be otherwise ? " Him, then, whom it is in
the power of another to restrain or to compel,
affirm confidently to be not free. And do not
mind his grandfathers, or great-grandfathers, or
inquire whether he hath been bought or sold ; but
if you hear him say from his heart, and with
emotion, My master, though twelve lictors should
march before him, call him a slave. And if you
should hear him say, Wretch that I am, what do
I suffer ! call him a slave. In short, if you see
him wailing, complaining, unprosperous, call him
a slave in purple. "Suppose, then, he doth
nothing of all this ?"—Do not yet say he is free,
but learn whether his principles are liable to compulsion, to restraint, or disappointment, and, if
you find this to be the case, call him a slave
keeping holiday during the Saturnalia. Say that
his master is abroad : he will come presently, and
you will know what he suffers. " Who will come?"
—Whoever hath the power either of bestowing or
taking away any of the things he wishes for.

E. D. iv. 1. 10.

A RE you free yourself, then? (it will be said).
By heaven, I wish and pray for it. But I
cannot yet face my masters. I still pay a regard
to my body, and set a great value on keeping it
whole, though at the same time it is not whole.
But I can show you one who was free, that you
may no longer seek an example. Diogenes was
free.—"How so?" Not because he was of free
parents, for he was not; but because he was so
himself, because he had cast away all the handles
of slavery, nor was there any way of getting at him,
nor anywhere to lay hold on him to enslave him.
Everything sat loose upon him, everything only
just hung on. If you took hold on his possessions, he would rather let them go than follow
you for them; if on his leg, he let go his leg; if
his body, he let go his body ; acquaintance.
friends. country, just the same. For he knew
whence he had them, and from whom and upon
what conditions he received them. But he would
never have forsaken his true parents the gods, and
his real country, nor have suffered anyone to be
more dutiful and obedient to them than he; nor
would anyone have died more readily for his
country than he.

E. D. iv. 1, 17.

$\mathcal{S}$PEAK the truth, slave, and do not run away from your masters, nor deny them, nor dare to assert your freedom when you have so many proofs of your slavery. One might indeed find some excuse for a person, compelled by love to do something contrary to his opinion, even when at the same time he sees what is best and yet hath not resolution enough to follow it, since he is withheld by something violent and, in some measure, divine. But who can bear you, who are in love with old men and women , and wipe their noses, and wash them, and bribe them with presents, and wait upon them when they are sick like a slave ; at the same time wishing they may die, and inquiring of the physician whether their distemper be yet mortal? And again, when for these great and venerable magistracies and honours you kiss the hands of the slaves of others, so that you are the slave of those who are not free themselves ! And then you walk about in state, a prætor, or a consul. Do not I know how you came to be prætor, whence you received the consulship, who gave it you? For my own part, I would not even live, if I must live by Felicio's means, and bear his pride and slavish insolence. For I know what a slave is, blinded by what he thinks good fortune.

E. D. IV. 1, 16.

SAITH the Poet, "The winds blow upon the trees, and their leaves fall upon the ground. Then do the trees begin to bud again, and by the springtime they put forth new branches. So is the generation of men; some come into the world, and others go out of it." Of these leaves then thy Children are. And they also that applaud thee so gravely, or, that applaud thy speeches, with that their usual acclamation, O wisely spoken! and speak well of thee, as on the other side, they that stick not to curse thee, they that privately and secretly dispraise and deride thee, they also are but leaves. And they also that shall follow, in whose memories the names of men famous after death, is preserved, they are but leaves neither. For even so is it of all these worldly things. Their spring comes, and they are put forth. Then blows the wind, and they go down. And then in lieu of them grow others out of the common matter of all things, like unto them. But, to endure but for a while, is common unto all. Why then shouldst thou so earnestly either seek after these things, or fly from them, as though they should endure for ever? Yet a little while, and thine eyes will be closed up, and for him that carries thee to thy grave shall another mourn within a while after.

M. A. x. 36.

A GOOD man is invincible ; for he doth not contend where he is not superior. If you would have his land, take it , take his servants, take his public post, take his body. But you will never frustrate his desire, nor make him incur his aversion. He engages in no combat but what concerns the objects of his own choice. How can he fail then to be invincible?

E. D. iii. 6, 2.

MERE wisdom, perhaps, is not a sufficient qualification for the care of youth. There ought to be likewise a certain readiness and aptitude for this, and, indeed, a particular constitution of body; and, above all, a counsel from God to undertake this office.

E. D iii. 21, 1

CHOOSE rather to have your children well instructed than rich.

Attributed to EPICTETUS.

THAT meekness is a thing unconquerable, if it be true and natural, and not affected, or hypocritical. For how shall even the most fierce and malicious that thou shalt conceive, be able to hold on against thee, if thou shalt still continue meek and loving unto him ; and that even at that time, when he is about to do thee wrong, thou shalt be well disposed, and in good temper, with all meekness to teach him, and to instruct him better? As for example; My son, we were not born for this, to hurt and annoy one another ; It will be thy hurt not mine, my son ; and so to show him forcibly and fully, that it is so in very deed : and that neither Bees do it to one another, nor any other creatures that are naturally sociable. But this thou must do, not scoffingly, not by way of exprobration, but tenderly without any harshness of words. Neither must thou do it by way of exercise, or ostentation, that they that are by and hear thee, may admire thee : but so always that nobody be privy to it, but himself alone . yea, though there be more present at the same time.

M. A. ix. 16.

A MAN is carried to prison. What hath happened? He is carried to prison. That he is unhappy, is an addition that everyone makes of his own.—But Zeus doth not order these things right. Why so? Because he hath made you patient? Because he hath made you brave? Because he hath made them to be no evils? Because it is permitted you, while you suffer them, to be happy? Because he hath opened you the door, whenever they do not suit you? Go out, man, and do not complain.

E. D. iii. 8, 2.

BEING asked what common sense was, he answered . As that may be called a common ear which distinguishes only sounds, but that which distinguishes notes an artistic one; so there are some things which men not totally perverted discern by their common natural powers; and such a disposition is called common sense.

E. D. iii. 6, 3.

AS the sun doth not wait for prayers and incantations to be prevailed on to rise, but immediately shines forth, and is received with universal salutation : so, neither do you wait for applauses and shouts and praises, in order to do good ; but be a voluntary benefactor, and you will be beloved like the sun.

E. FR. 83.

WHEN it is our duty to share the danger of a friend or of our country, we ought not to consult the oracle whether we shall share it with them or not. For, though the diviner should forewarn you that the victims are unfavourable, this means no more than that either death or mutilation or exile is portended. But we have reason within us, and it directs, even with these hazards, to stand by our friend and our country. Attend, therefore, to the greater diviner, the Pythian god, who cast out of the temple the person who gave no assistance to his friend while another was murdering him.

E. M. 32.

THERE is not any man that is so happy in his death, but that some of those that are by him when he dies, will be ready to rejoice at his supposed calamity. Is it one that was virtuous and wise indeed? Will there not someone or other be found, who thus will say to himself, Well now at last shall I be at rest from this Pedagogue ? He did not indeed otherwise trouble us much, but I know well enough that in his heart, he did much condemn us. Thus will they speak of the virtuous.

M. A. x. 36.

REMEMBER that all is but opinion, and all opinion depends of the mind. Take thine opinion away, and then as a ship that hath stricken in within the arms and mouth of the harbour, a present calm ; all things safe and steady ; a Bay, not capable of any storms and tempests : as the Poet hath it

M. A. xii. 16.

H E who is greedy of credit and reputation after his death, doth not consider, that they themselves by whom he is remembered, shall soon after every one of them be dead · And they likewise that succeed those; until at last all memory, which hitherto by the succession of men admiring and soon after dying hath had its course, be quite extinct. But suppose that both they that shall remember thee, and thy memory with them should be immortal, what is that to thee? I will not say to thee after thou art dead, but even to thee living, what is thy praise? That which is fair and goodly, whatsoever it be, and in what respect soever it be, that it is fair and goodly, it is so of itself, and terminates in itself, not admitting praise as a part or member; that therefore which is praised, is not thereby made either better or worse. This I understand even of those things, that are commonly called fair and good, as those which are commended either for the matter itself, or for curious workmanship. As for that which is truly good, what can it stand in need of more, than either Justice or Truth; or more than either kindness and modesty? Which of all those, either becomes good or fair, because commended; or dispraised suffers any damage?

M. A. iv. 16.

BUT the care of thine honour and reputation will perchance distract thee. How can that be, if thou dost look back, and consider both how quickly all things that are, are forgotten, and what an immense chaos of eternity was before, and will follow after all things : and the vanity of praise, and the inconstancy and variableness of human Judgments and opinions, and the narrowness of the place, wherein it is limited and circumscribed? For the whole earth is but as one point; and of it, this inhabited part of it, is but a very little part; and of this part, how many in number, and what manner of men are they, that will commend thee? What remains then, but that thou often put in practice this kind of retiring of thyself, to this little part of thyself; and above all things, keep thyself from distraction, and intend not anything vehemently, but be free and consider all things, as a man, whose proper object is virtue, as a man, whose true nature is to be kind and sociable, as a Citizen, as a mortal creature.

M. A. iv. 3.

WHATSOEVER any man either doth or saith, thou must be good; not for any man's sake, but for thine own nature's sake.

M. A. vii. 12.

AFTER one consideration, man is nearest unto us; as we are bound to do them good, and to bear with them. But as he may oppose any of our true proper actions, so man is unto me but as a thing indifferent: even as the sun, or the wind, or some wild beast. By some of these it may be, that some operation or other of mine, may be hindered; however, of my mind and resolution itself, there can be no let or impediment.

M. A. v. 17.

WE ought to do well by our friends when they are present, and speak well of them when they are absent.

Attributed to EPICTETUS.

WHAT is it that we must bestow our care and
diligence upon? even upon this only : That
our minds and wills be just; that our actions be
charitable; that our speech be never deceitful, or
that our understanding be not subject to error;
that our inclination be always set to embrace
whatsoever shall happen unto us, as necessary, as
usual, as ordinary, as flowing from such a beginning, and such a fountain, from which both thou
thyself, and all things are.

M. A. iv. 28.

ENDEAVOUR to continue such, as philosophy
(hadst thou wholly and constantly applied
thyself unto it) would have made and secured thee.
Worship the gods, procure the welfare of men,
this life is short. Charitable actions, and a holy
disposition, is the only fruit of this mortal life.

M. A. vi. 27.

BE willing to approve yourself to yourself. Be willing to appear beautiful in the sight of God : be desirous to converse in purity with your own pure mind, and with God ; and then, if any such appearance strikes you, Plato directs you : " Have recourse to expiations go a suppliant to the temples of the averting deities." It is sufficient, however, if you propose to yourself the example of wise and good men, whether alive or dead ; and compare your conduct with theirs.

E. D. 11. 18, 4.

BUT you set up for a physician, provided with
nothing but medicines, and without knowing,
or having studied, where or how they are to be applied. "Why, such a one had medicines for the
eyes, and I have the same." Have you, then, a
faculty too of making use of them? Do you at
all know when and how and to whom they will
be of service?

E. D. iii 21, 1.

HIPPOCRATES having cured many sicknesses,
fell sick himself and died. The Chaldeans
and Astrologians having foretold the deaths of
divers, were afterwards themselves surprised by
the fates. Alexander and Pompeius, and Caius
Cæsar, having destroyed so many towns, and cut
off in the field so many thousands both of horse
and foot, yet they themselves at last, were fain to
part with their own lives. Heraclitus having written so many natural tracts concerning the last and
general conflagration of the world, died afterwards
all filled with water within, and all bedaubed with
dirt and dung without. Lice killed Democritus;
and Socrates, another sort of vermin, wicked un-
godly men

M. A. ii. 3.

A CARPENTER doth not come and say,
"Hear me discourse on the art of building";
but he hires a house and fits it up and shows himself master of his trade.   Let it be your business
likewise to do something like this : eat like a man ;
drink, dress, marry, have children, perform the duty
of a citizen ; bear reproach ; bear with an unreasonable brother ; bear with a father ; bear with a son,
a neighbour, a companion, as becomes a man.
Show us these things that we may see that you
have really learnt somewhat from the philosophers.

E. D. iii. 21, 1.

THE brass pot and the earthen pitcher, the
fable says, are an unsuitable match.

E. D. iii. 12, 2.

NEVER call yourself a philosopher, nor talk a great deal among the unlearned about philosophic principles, but act conformably to them. Thus, at an entertainment, do not talk how persons ought to eat, but eat as you ought. For remember that in this manner Socrates also universally avoided all ostentation. And when persons came to him and desired to be recommended by him to philosophers, he took and recommended them, so well did he bear being overlooked. And, if anyone tells you that you know nothing, and you are not nettled at it, then you may be sure that you have begun your business. For sheep do not throw up the grass to show the shepherds how much they have eaten , but, inwardly digesting their food, they outwardly produce wool and milk. Thus, therefore, do you likewise not show theorems to the unlearned, but the actions produced by them after they have been digested.

E. M. 46.

Un   · ®

EUPHRATES was in the right to say, "I long endeavoured to conceal my embracing the philosophic life, and it was of use to me. For, in the first place, I knew that what I did right I did it not for spectators, but for myself. I ate in a proper manner for myself. I had a composed look and walk, all for God and myself. Then, as I fought alone, I was alone in danger. Philosophy was in no danger, on my doing anything shameful or unbecoming, nor did I hurt the rest of the world, which, by offending as a philosopher, I might have done. For this reason, they who were ignorant of my intention used to wonder, that while I conversed and lived entirely with philosophers, I never took up the character. And where was the harm, that I should be discovered to be a philosopher by my actions and not by the usual badges?"

E. D. iv. 8, 4.

SUCH a one is a philosopher. Why? Because he wears a cloak and long hair. What, then, do mountebanks wear? And so, when people see any of these acting indecently, they presently say, "See what the philosopher doth." But they ought rather, from his acting indecently, to say he is no philosopher.

E. D. iv. 8, 1.

AS soon as they have put on a cloak and let their beard grow they cry, "I am a philosopher." Yet no one says, "I am a musician," because he hath bought a fiddle and fiddlestick; nor, "I am a smith," because he is dressed in the Vulcanian cap and apron. But they take their name from their art, not from their habit.

E. D. iv. 8, 3.

JULY I

A S bad performers cannot sing alone but in a chorus, so some persons cannot walk alone. If you are anything, walk alone, talk by yourself, and do not skulk in the chorus. Think a little at last; look about you, sift yourself, that you may know what you are.

E. D. iii. 14, 1.

T HOU art now ready to die, and yet hast thou not attained to that perfect simplicity: thou art yet subject to many troubles, and perturbations; not yet free from all fear and suspicion of external accidents; nor yet either so meekly disposed towards all men, as thou shouldst; or so affected as one, whose only study, and only wisdom is, to be just in all his actions.

M. A. iv. 3.

183

WE ought, however, to be prepared in some manner for this also, to be self-sufficient and able to bear our own company. For as Jupiter converses with himself, acquiesces in himself, and contemplates his own administration, and is employed in thoughts worthy of himself: so should we too be able to talk with ourselves, and not to need the conversation of others, nor be at a loss for employment; to attend to the divine administration; to consider our relation to other beings; how we have formerly been affected by events, how we are affected now; what are the things that still press upon us, how these too may be cured, how removed; if anything wants completing, to complete it according to reason.

E. D. iii. 13, 1.

I F a person drinks water, or doth anything else for the sake of exercise, upon every occasion he tells all he meets, "I drink water." Why, do you drink water merely for the sake of drinking it? If it doth you any good to drink it, drink it; if not, you act ridiculously. But, if it is for your advantage, and you drink it, say nothing about it before those who are apt to take offence. What then? These are the very people you wish to please.

E. D. iii. 14, 2.

WHAT art, and profession soever thou hast learned, endeavour to affect it, and comfort thyself in it; and pass the remainder of thy life as one who from his whole heart commits himself and whatsoever belongs unto him, unto the gods, and as for men, carry not thyself either tyrannically or servilely towards any.

M. A. iv. 26.

WE would live immediately as men already wise, and be of service to mankind.—Of what service? What are you doing? Why, have you been of service to yourself? But you would exhort them. You exhort! Would you be of service to them, show them, by your own example, what kind of men philosophy makes, and be not impertinent. When you eat, be of service to those who eat with you; when you drink, to those who drink with you. Be of service to them, by giving way to all, yielding to them, bearing with them; and not by throwing out your own ill humour upon them.

E. D. iii. 13, 3.

THERE is, who without so much as a Coat; and there is, who without so much as a book, doth put philosophy in practice. I am half naked, neither have I bread to eat, and yet I depart not from Reason, saith one. But I say; I want the food of good teaching, and instructions, and yet I depart not from Reason.

M A. iv. 25.

186

LET not him think he is loved by any who loves none

Attributed to EPICTETUS.

DEATH hangs over thee : whilst thou livest, whilst thou mayest, be good.

M. A. iv. 14.

LOOK not about upon the evil conditions of others, but run on straight in the line.

M. A. iv. 15.

WHAT you avoid suffering yourself, attempt not to impose on others.

E. FR. 38.

COMMUNICATE to strangers and persons in need, according to your ability. For he who gives nothing to the needy, shall receive nothing in his own need.

E. FR. 103.

L ET not the general representation unto thyself
of the wretchedness of this our mortal life,
trouble thee.   Let not thy mind wander up and
down, and heap together in her thoughts, the
many troubles and grievous calamities which thou
art as subject unto as any other.   But as everything in particular doth happen, put this question
unto thyself, and say; What is it that in this
present matter, seems unto thee so intolerable?
For thou wilt be ashamed to confess it.   Then
upon this presently call to mind, that neither that
which is future, nor that which is past can hurt
thee; but that only which is present. (And that
also is much lessened, if thou dost rightly circumscribe it) and then check thy mind if for so
little a while, (a mere instant) it cannot hold out
with patience.

M. A. viii. 34.

EVERY place is safe to him who lives with justice.

E. FR. 97

SO live as indifferent to the world, and all worldly objects, as one who liveth by himself alone upon some desert hill. For whether here, or there, if the whole world be but as one Town, it matters not much for the place.

M. A. x. 17.

WHATSOEVER doth happen in the world, doth happen justly, and so if thou dost well take heed, thou shalt find it. I say not only in right order by a series of inevitable consequences, but according to Justice and as it were by way of equal distribution, according to the true worth of everything. Continue then to take notice of it, as thou hast begun, and whatsoever thou doest, do it not without this proviso, that it be a thing of that nature that a good man, (as the word good is properly taken) may do it. This observe carefully in every action.

M. A iv. 8.

Un   ℗

WHY, then, are you anxious? Why do you keep yourself waking? Why do not you calculate where your good and evil lies; and say they are both in my own power, neither can any deprive me of the one, or involve me, against my will, in the other? Why, then, do not I lay myself down and snore? What is my own is safe. Let what belongs to others look to itself who carries it off, how it is given away by him that hath the disposal of it. Who am I, to will that it should be so and so? For is the option given to me? Hath anyone made me the dispenser of it? What I have in my own disposal is enough for me. I must make the best I can of this. Other things must be as the master of them pleases.

E. D. iv. 9, 4.

IF in this kind of life thy body be able to hold out, it is a shame that thy soul should faint first, and give over. Take heed lest of a philosopher thou become a mere Cæsar in time, and receive a new tincture from the Court. For it may happen if thou dost not take heed. Keep thyself, therefore, truly simple, good, sincere, grave, free from all ostentation, a lover of that which is just, religious, kind, tender-hearted, strong and vigorous to undergo anything that becomes thee.

M. A. vi. 27.

DEATH is a cessation from the impressions of the senses, the tyranny of the passions, the errors of the mind, and the servitude of the body.

M. A. vi. 26.

IF you would be good, first believe that you are bad.

E. FR. 2.

WHAT is it then that doth keep thee here, if things sensible be so mutable and un-settled? and the senses so obscure, and so fallible? and our souls nothing but an exhalation of blood? and to be in credit among such, be but vanity? What is it that thou dost stay for? an Extinction, or a Translation; either of them with a propitious and contented mind. But till that time come, what will content thee? what else, but to worship and praise the Gods; and to do good unto men. To bear with them, and to forbear to do them any wrong. And for all external things belonging either to this thy wretched body, or life, to remember that they are neither thine, nor in thy power.

M. A. v. 27.

A MAN must know many things first, before he be able truly and judiciously to judge of another man's action.

M. A. ix. 16.

IF anyone tells you that such a person speaks ill of you, do not make excuses about what is said of you, but answer: "He doth not know my other faults, else he would not have mentioned only these."

E. M. 33.

OUT of Antisthenes. "It is a princely thing to do well, and to be ill spoken of. It is a shameful thing that the face should be subject unto the mind, to be put into what shape it will, and to be dressed by it as it will, and that the mind should not bestow so much care upon herself, as to fashion herself, and to dress herself as best becometh her."

M. A. vii. 24.

OLYMPIAN ZEUS doth not lift up his brow, but keeps a steady countenance, as becomes him who is about to say—

"The immutable decree
No force can shake : what is, that ought to be."
POPE.

"Such will I show myself to you : faithful, modest, noble, tranquil."—What, and immortal too, and exempt from age and sickness?—"No. But sickening and dying as becomes a god. This is in my power ; this I can do. The other is not in my power, nor can I do it." Shall I show you the sinews of a philosopher?

What are they?

A desire undisappointed : an aversion unincurred : pursuits duly exerted : a careful resolution : an unerring assent. These you shall see.

E. D. ii. 8, 4.

Un   · ®

SHOW me that you are faithful, a man of honour, steady; show me that you have friendly principles; show me that your vessel is not leaky, and you shall see that I will not stay till you have trusted your affairs to me; but I will come and entreat you to hear an account of mine. For who would not make use of a good vessel? Who despises a benevolent and friendly adviser? Who will not gladly receive one to share the burden of his difficulties, and by sharing to make it lighter? "Well, but I trust you, and you do not trust me." You do not really trust me: but you are a blab, and therefore can keep nothing in. For if the former be the case, trust only me. But now, whoever you see at leisure, you sit down by him and say: "My dear friend, there is not a man in the world that wishes me better, or hath more kindness for me than you: I entreat you to hear my affairs."

E. D. iv. 13, 3.

WHEN one hath safely entrusted his secrets to me, shall I, in imitation of him, trust mine to anyone who comes in my way? The case is different. I indeed hold my tongue (supposing me to be of such a disposition), but he goes and discovers them to everybody; and then, when I come to find it out, if I happen to be like him, from a desire of revenge I discover his, and asperse, and am aspersed. But, if I remember that one man doth not hurt another, but that everyone is hurt and profited by his own actions, I indeed keep to this, not to do anything like him; yet, by my own talkative folly, I suffer what I do suffer.

"Ay, but it is unfair, when you have heard the secrets of your neighbour, not to communicate anything to him in return."—"Why, did I ask you to do it, sir? Did you tell me your affairs upon condition that I should tell you mine in return? If you are a blab, and believe all you meet to be friends, would you have me, too, become like you? But what if the case be this: that you did right in trusting your affairs to me, but it is not right that I should trust you? Would you have me run headlong and fall? This is just as if I had a sound barrel and you a leaky one, and you should come and deposit your wine with me to put it into my barrel, and then should take it ill that in my turn I did not trust you with my wine. No. You have a leaky barrel."

E. D. iv. 13, 2, 3.

MAN is made for fidelity, and whoever subverts this subverts the peculiar property of man.

E. D. II. 4, I.

IT is good to know your own qualifications and powers; that, where you are not qualified, you may be quiet, and not angry that others have the advantage of you in such things.

E. D. ii. 6, I.

WHAT is the first business of one who studies philosophy? To part with self-conceit. For it is impossible for anyone to begin to learn what he hath a conceit that he already knows.

E. D. ii. 17, I.

THERE is nothing more shameful than perfidious friendship. Above all things, that must be avoided. However, true goodness, simplicity, and kindness cannot so be hidden, but that as we have already said in the very eyes and countenance they will show themselves.

M. A. xi. 7.

Un   ®

LET it not be in any man's power, to say truly of thee, that thou art not truly simple, or, sincere and open, or not good. Let him be deceived whosoever he be that shall have any such opinion of thee. For all this doth depend of thee. For who is it that should hinder thee from being either truly simple or good? Do thou only resolve rather not to live, than not to be such.

M. A. x. 33.

HOW rotten and insincere is he, that saith, I am resolved to carry myself hereafter towards you with all ingenuity and simplicity. O man, what dost thou mean! What needs this profession of thine? It ought to be written upon thy forehead.

M. A. xi. 14.

AT the conceit and apprehension that such and such a one hath sinned, thus reason with thyself, What do I know whether this be a sin indeed, as it seems to be? But if it be, what do I know but that he himself hath already condemned himself for it? And that is all one as if a man should scratch and tear his own face, an object of compassion rather than of anger.

M. A. xii. 12.

WHEN any person doth ill by you, or speaks ill of you, remember that he acts or speaks from a supposition of its being his duty. Now, it is not possible that he should follow what appears right to you, but what appears so to himself. Therefore, if he judges from a wrong appearance, he is the person hurt, since he too is the person deceived. For if anyone should suppose a true proposition to be false, the proposition is not hurt, but he who is deceived about it.

E. M. 42.

IT is better to offend seldom (owning it when we do), and act often wisely, than to say we seldom err, and offend frequently.

E. FR. 3.

BUT if it be somewhat that is amiss in thine own disposition, that doth grieve thee, mayest thou not rectify thy moral tenets and opinions. But if it grieve thee, that thou dost not perform that which seemeth unto thee right and just, why dost not thou choose rather to perform it than to grieve? But somewhat that is stronger than thyself doth hinder thee. Let it not grieve thee then, if it be not thy fault that the thing is not performed. Yea but it is a thing of that nature, as that thy life is not worth the while, except it may be performed. If it be so, upon condition that thou be kindly and lovingly disposed towards all men, thou mayest be gone. For even then, as much as at any time, art thou in a very good estate of performance, when thou dost die in charity with those, that are an obstacle unto thy performance.

M A. viii. 45.

THERE are some things which men confess with ease; others, with difficulty. No one, for instance, will confess himself a fool, or a blockhead; but, on the contrary, you will hear everyone say, "I wish my fortune was equal to my mind." But they easily confess themselves fearful, and say, "I am somewhat timorous, I confess, but in other respects you will not find me a fool." No one will easily confess himself intemperate in his desires; upon no account dishonest, nor absolutely very envious, or meddling; but many confess themselves to have the weakness of being compassionate.

E. D. ii. 21, 1.

WHAT is the reason of all this? The principal is, an inconsistency and confusion in what relates to good and evil. But different people have different inducements. In general, whatever they imagine to be base they do not absolutely confess Fear and compassion they imagine to belong to a well-meaning disposition ; but stupidity to a slave. Offences against society they do not own ; but, in most faults, they are brought to a confession chiefly from imagining that there is something involuntary in them, as in fear and compassion. And, though a person should in some measure confess himself intemperate in his desires, he accuses his passion, and expects forgiveness as for an involuntary fault. But dishonesty is not imagined to be, by any means, involuntary. In jealousy, too, there is something, they suppose, of involuntary ; and this likewise, in some degree, they confess.

E. D. ii. 21, 1.

THERE are some whom there is no convincing.
So that now I think I understand what before
I did not, the meaning of that common saying,
that a fool will neither bend nor break. May it
never fall to my lot to have a wise, that is an
intractable, fool for my friend. "It is all to no
purpose: I am determined." So are madmen
too; but the more strongly they are determined
upon absurdities, the more need have they of
hellebore. Why will you not act like a sick
person, and apply yourself to a physician? "Sir,
I am sick Give me your assistance · consider
what I am to do. It is my part to follow your
directions." So, in the present case, I know not
what I ought to do; and I am come to learn.

F. D. ii. 15, 2.

Un   · ®

"NO; but talk to me about other things; for upon this I am determined." What other things? What is of greater consequence than to convince you that it is not sufficient to be determined, and to persist? This is the tension of a madman, not of one in health. "I will die if you compel me to this." Why so, man: what is the matter?—"I am determined." I have a lucky escape that you are not determined to kill me. "I take no money." Why so? "I am determined." Be assured that with that very tension which you now make use of to refuse it, you may very possibly, hereafter, have as unreasonable a propensity to take it; and again to say, "I am determined" As in a distempered and rheumatic body the humour tends sometimes to one part, sometimes to another; thus it is uncertain which way a sickly mind will incline. But if to its inclination and bent an obstinate tension be likewise added, the evil then becomes desperate and incurable.

E. D. ii. 15, 2.

HE, then, is an able speaker, and excels at once in exhortation and conviction, who can discover to each man the contradiction by which he errs, and prove clearly to him, that what he would, he doth not; and what he would not do, that he doth. For if that be shown, he will depart from it of his own accord: but till you have shown it, be not surprised that he remains where he is: for he doth it on the appearance that he acts rightly. Hence Socrates, relying on this faculty, used to say, "It is not my custom to cite any other witness of my assertions, but I am always contented with my opponent. I call and summon him for my witness; and his single evidence is instead of all others." For he knew that if a rational soul be moved by anything, the scale must turn whether it will or no. Show the governing faculty of reason a contradiction, and it will renounce it: but, till you have shown it, rather blame yourself than him who is unconvinced.

E. D. ii. 26, 2.

EITHER teach them, or bear with them.

M. A.

"AM I to blame, then, sir, and ignorant of my
duty and of what is incumbent on me? If
this is neither to be learnt nor taught, why do you
find fault with me? If it is to be taught, pray
teach me yourself; or, if you cannot, give me
leave to learn it from those who profess to understand it. Besides: do you think that I voluntarily
fall into evil, and miss of good? Heaven forbid!
What, then, is the cause of my faults?"—Ignorance. "Are you not willing, then, that I should
get rid of my ignorance? Who was ever taught
the art of music or navigation by anger? Do you
expect, then, that your anger should teach me the
art of living?"

E. D. i. 26, 1.

WHY do not you, as we pity the blind and lame, so likewise pity those who are blinded and lamed in their superior faculties? Whoever, therefore, duly remembers that the appearance of things to the mind is the standard of every action to man : that this is either right or wrong · and, if right, he is without fault, if wrong, he himself bears the punishment; for that one man cannot be the person deceived, and another the sufferer : will not be outrageous and angry at anyone; will not revile, or reproach, or hate, or quarrel with anyone.

E. D. i. 28, 2.

IS the cucumber bitter? set it away. Brambles are in the way? avoid them. Let this suffice. Add not presently speaking unto thyself, What serve these things for in the world? For, this, one that is acquainted with the mysteries of Nature, will laugh at thee for it; as a Carpenter would or a Shoemaker, if meeting in either of their shops with some shavings, or small remnants of their work, thou shouldst blame them for it.

M. A. viii. 48.

IN another man's mind and understanding thy
evil cannot subsist, nor in any proper temper
or distemper of the natural constitution of thy
body, which is but as it were the coat, or cottage
of thy soul. Wherein then, but in that part of
thee, wherein the conceit, and apprehension of
any misery can subsist? Let not that part therefore admit any such conceit, and then all is well.
Though thy body which is so near it, should either
be cut or burnt, or suffer any corruption, or putrefaction, yet let that part to which it belongs to
judge of these, be still at rest; that is, Let her
judge this, that, whatsoever it is, that equally may
happen to a wicked man, and to a good man, is
neither good, nor evil. For that which happens
equally to him that lives according to Nature,
and to him that doth not, is neither according
to nature, nor against it, and by consequence,
neither good, nor bad.

M. A. iv. 32.

DOTH any man offend? It is against himself that he doth offend: why should it trouble thee?

M. A. iv. 21.

ONE thing there is, and that only, which is worth our while in this World, and ought by as much to be esteemed; and that is, according to truth and righteousness, meekly and lovingly to converse with false, and unrighteous men.

M. A. vi. 42.

WHEN thou wilt comfort and cheer thyself, call to mind the several gifts and virtues of them, whom thou dost daily converse with; as for example, the industry of the one; the modesty of another; the liberality of a third; of another some other thing. For nothing can so much rejoice thee, as the resemblances and parallels of several virtues, visible and eminent in the dispositions of those who live with thee.

M. A. vi. 43.

Un   ®

WHEN any shall either impeach thee with false accusations, or hatefully reproach thee, or shall use any such carriage towards thee, get thee presently to their minds and understandings, and look in them, and behold what manner of men they be. Thou shalt see that there is no such occasion why it should trouble thee, what such as they think of thee. Yet must thou love them still, for by nature they are thy friends.

M. A. ix. 25.

IF it were thine act and in thine own power, why wouldst thou do it? If it were not, whom dost thou accuse? the atoms, or the gods? For to do either, is the part of a madman. Thou must therefore blame nobody, but if it be in thy power, redress what is amiss; if it be not, to what end dost thou complain?

M. A. viii. 15.

210

Un ℝ

WHEN thou art offended with any man's transgression, presently reflect upon thyself, and consider what thou thyself art guilty of in the same kind.

M. A. x. 30.

WHENSOEVER any man doth trespass against thee, presently consider with thyself what it was that he did suppose to be good, what to be evil, when he did trespass. For this when thou knowest, thou wilt pity him; thou wilt have no occasion either to wonder, or to be angry. For either thou thyself dost yet live in that error and ignorance, as that thou dost suppose either that very thing that he doth, or some other like worldly thing, to be good; and so thou art bound to pardon him if he have done that which thou in the like case wouldst have done thyself. Or if so be that thou dost not any more suppose the same things to be good or evil, that he doth; how canst thou but be gentle unto him that is in an error?

M. A. vii. 19.

I F you are hasty, man, let it be your exercise to bear ill language patiently ; and when you are affronted, not to be angry.

E. D. iii. 12, 2.

B UT if this be done for mere ostentation, it belongs to one who looks out and hunts for something external, and seeks for spectators to exclaim, "What a great man !" Hence Apollonius said well: "If you have a mind to exercise yourself for your own benefit, when you are choking with heat, take a little cold water in your mouth and spirt it out again, and tell nobody."

E. D. iii. 12, 5.

A N angry countenance is much against nature, and it is oftentimes the proper countenance of them that are at the point of death

M. A. vii. 18.

WHAT is it to be reviled, for instance? Stand by a stone and revile it; and what will you get? If you, therefore, would hear like a stone, what would your reviler be the better? But if the reviler hath the weakness of the reviled for an advantage ground, then he carries his point. "Strip him."—"What do you mean by him?" "Take my clothes; strip off them if you will. "I have put an affront upon you."—"Much good may it do you."

E. D. i. 25, 3.

WHAT is it then that should be dear unto us? to hear a clattering noise? if not that, then neither to be applauded by the tongues of men. For the praises of many tongues, is in effect no better, than the clattering of so many tongues. If then neither applause, what is there remaining that should be dear unto thee? This I think: that in all thy motions and actions thou be moved, and restrained according to thine own true natural constitution and construction only.

M. A. vi 15.

AUGUST I

IF you go and revile your brother, I tell you you
have forgot who you are, and what is your
name. For even if you were a smith and made
an ill use of the hammer, you would have forgot
the smith : and, if you have forgot the brother,
and are become, instead of a brother, an enemy
do you imagine you have made no change of one
thing for another in that case? If, instead of a
man, a gentle social creature, you are become
a wild beast, mischievous, insidious, biting; have
you lost nothing? But must you lose money, in
order to suffer damage; and is there no other
thing, the loss of which damages a man? If
you were to part with your skill in grammar, or
in music, would you think the loss of these a
damage? But if you part with honour, decency,
and gentleness, do you think that no matter?

E. D. ii. 10, 4.

WHY is it that they have railed at you? Because every man hates what hinders him. They would have one actor crowned, you another. They hindered you; and you, them. You proved the stronger. They have done what they could; they have railed at the person who hindered them. What would you have, then? Would you do as you please, and not have them even talk as they please? Where is the wonder of all this? Doth not the husbandman rail at Zeus when he is hindered by him? Doth not the sailor? Do men ever cease railing at Cæsar? What then, is Zeus ignorant of this? Are not the things that are said reported to Cæsar? How then doth he act? He knows that if he was to punish all railers, he would have nobody left to command.

E. D. iii. 5, 2.

Un   · ®

WILL you say, Hath no one any regard for me, a man of letters? Why, you are wicked, and fit for no use. Just as if wasps should take it ill that no one hath any regard for them, but all shun, and whoever can beats them down. You have such a sting, that whoever you strike with it is thrown into troubles and pangs. What would you have us do with you?

E. D. ii. 4, 1.

EITHER teach them better if it be in thy power; or if it be not, remember that for this use, to bear with them patiently, was mildness and goodness granted unto thee. The gods themselves are good unto such; yea and in some things, (as in matter of health, of wealth, of honour), are content often to further their endeavours : so good and gracious are they. And mightest thou not be so too? or, tell me, what doth hinder thee?

M. A. ix. 9.

HIM that offends, teach with love and meekness, and show him his error. But if thou canst not, then blame thyself, or rather not thyself neither, if thy will and endeavours have not been wanting

M. A. x. 4.

THEY are thieves and pilferers.

What do you mean by thieves and pilferers? They are in an error concerning good and evil. Ought you, then, to be angry, or to pity them? Do but show them their error, and you will see that they will amend their faults: but if they do not see it the principles they form are to them their supreme rule.

What then, ought not this thief and this adulterer to be destroyed?

By no means ask that: but say rather, "Ought not he to be destroyed who errs and is deceived in things of the greatest importance: blinded, not in the sight that distinguishes white from black, but in the judgment that distinguishes good from evil?" By stating your question thus you see how inhuman it is, and just as if you would say, "Ought not this blind, or that deaf man to be destroyed?" For, if the greatest hurt be a deprivation of the most valuable things, and the most valuable thing to everyone is a right judgment in choosing: when anyone is deprived of this, why, after all, are you angry? You ought not to be affected, man, contrary to nature, by the ills of another. Pity him rather. Do not be angry; nor say, as many do, What shall these execrable and odious wretches dare to act thus? Whence have you so suddenly learnt wisdom? Because we admire those things which such people take from us. Do not admire your clothes, and you will not be angry with the thief.

E. D. i. 18. 1.

TO desire things impossible is the part of a madman. But it is a thing impossible, that
wicked man should not commit some such things.
Neither doth anything happen to any man, which
in the ordinary course of nature as natural unto
him doth not happen. Again, the same things
happen unto others also. And truly, if either be
that is ignorant that such a thing hath happened
unto him, or he that is ambitious to be commended for his magnanimity, can be patient and
is not grieved: is it not a grievous thing, that
either ignorance or a vain desire to please and
to be commended, should be more powerful and
effectual than true prudence? As for the things
themselves, they touch not the soul, neither can
they have any access unto it, neither can they
of themselves anywise either affect it, or move it.

M A. v 16.

A WISE and good person neither quarrels with anyone himself nor so far as possible, suffers another. The life of Socrates affords us an example of this too. For he well remembered that no one is master of the ruling faculty of another, and therefore desired nothing but what was his own. "And what is that?" Not that this or that person should be moved conformably to nature, for that belongs to others; but that while they act in their own way as they please, he should nevertheless be affected and live according to nature.

E. D. iv 5, 1.

THE best kind of revenge is, not to become like unto them.

Let this be thy only joy, and thy only comfort, from one sociable kind action without intermission to pass unto another, God being ever in thy mind.

M. A. vi. 5, 6.

IF he have sinned, his is the harm, not mine. But perchance he hath not.

M. A. ix. 37.

220

EPICTETUS being asked how a person might grieve his enemy, answered, "By doing as well as possible himself."

E. FR. 125.

HE that is unjust, is also impious. For the Nature of the Universe, having made all reasonable creatures one for another, to the end that they should do one another good : more or less according to the several persons and occasions, but in no wise hurt one another: it is manifest that he that doth transgress against this her will, is guilty of impiety towards the most ancient and venerable of all the Deities.

M. A. ix. 1.

THOSE things that are his own, and in his own power, he himself takes order for that they be good: and as for those that happen unto him, he believes them to be so.

M. A. iii. 4.

SOME are peevish and fastidious, and say, I cannot dine with such a fellow, to be obliged to hear him all day recounting how he fought in Mysia. "I told you, my friend, how I gained the eminence. There I am besieged again." But another says, "I had rather get a dinner, and hear him prate as much as he pleases."

Do you compare the value of these things, and judge for yourself; but do not let it be with depression and anxiety, and with a supposition that you are unhappy, for no one compels you to go.

E. D. i. 25, 3.

RECEIVE temporal blessings without ostentation, when they are sent, and thou shalt be able to part with them with all readiness and facility when they are taken from thee again.

M. Λ. viii. 31.

HOW is my brother to lay aside his anger against me?

Bring him to me, and I will tell him; but I have nothing to say to you about his anger.

E. D. i. 15, 1.

AFTER this, know likewise, that you are a brother; and that to this character it belongs, to make concessions; to be easily persuaded ; to use gentle language; never to claim for yourself any of the things dependent on choice, but cheerfully to give these, that you may have the larger share of what is dependent on it.   For consider what it is, instead of a lettuce, for instance, or a chair, to procure for yourself a good temper?   How great an advantage gained !

E. D ii. 10, 3.

ONE prayeth how he may be rid of such a one : pray thou that thou mayest so patiently bear with him, as that thou have no such need to be rid of him.

M. A. ix. 40.

WHEN at any time thou art offended with anyone's impudence, put presently this question to thyself. What? Is it then possible, that there should not be any impudent men in the world! Certainly it is not possible. Desire not then that which is impossible. For this one (thou must think), whosoever he be, is one of those impudent ones, that the world cannot be without. So of the subtle and crafty, so of the perfidious, so of everyone that offendeth, must thou ever be ready to reason with thyself. For whilst in general thou dost thus reason with thyself, that the kind of them must needs be in the world, thou wilt be the better able to use meekness towards every particular. This also thou shalt find of very good use, upon every such occasion, presently to consider with thyself, what proper virtue nature hath furnished man with, against such a vice, or to encounter with a disposition vicious in this kind. As for example, against the unthankful, it hath given goodness and meekness, as an antidote, and so against another vicious in another kind some other peculiar faculty. And generally, is it not in thy power to instruct him better, that is in an error ?

M A. ix. 43.

CHASTISE your passions, that they may not punish you.

E. FR. 4.

THERE are some punishments appointed, as by a law, for such as disobey the divine administration. Whoever shall esteem anything good, except what depends on choice, let him envy, let him covet, let him flatter, let him be full of perturbation. Whoever esteems anything else to be evil, let him grieve, let him mourn, let him lament, let him be wretched. And yet, though thus severely punished, we cannot desist.

E. D. iii. 11, 1.

WHENSOEVER thou findest thyself, that thou art in danger of a relapse, and that thou art not able to master and overcome those difficulties and temptations that present themselves in thy present station : get thee into any private corner, where thou mayest be better able. Or if that will not serve, forsake even thy life rather. But so that it be not in passion, but in a plain voluntary modest way this being the only commendable action of thy whole life, that thus thou art departed, or this having been the main work and business of thy whole life, that thou mightest thus depart.

M. A. x. 5.

Un   ·®

IS there not a divine and powerful and inevitable law which exacts the greatest punishments
from those who are guilty of the greatest offences?
For what says this law? Let him who claims
what doth not belong to him be arrogant, be vain-
glorious, be base, be a slave; let him grieve, let
him envy, let him pity. and, in a word, let him
be unhappy, let him lament.

E. D. iii. 24, 2.

HE that sinneth, sinneth unto himself. He
that is unjust, hurts himself, in that he
makes himself worse than he was before. Not
he only that committeth, but he also that omitteth
something, is oftentimes unjust.

M A. ix. 4.

GOVERN us like reasonable creatures   Show us what is for our interest, and we will pursue it; show us what is against our interest, and we will avoid it.   Like Socrates, make us imitators of yourself.   He was properly a governor of men, who subjected their desires and aversions, their pursuits, their avoidances, to himself.   " Do this ; do not do that, or I will throw you into prison " Going thus far only is not governing men like reasonable creatures.   But—"Do as Zeus hath commanded, or you will be punished.   You will be a loser."

What shall I lose?

Nothing more than the not doing what you ought.   You will lose your fidelity, honour, decency.   Look for no greater losses than these.

E. D. iii. 7, 2.

Un   ·ℝ

IT is better, by yielding to truth, to conquer opinion , than, by yielding to opinion, to be defeated by truth.

E FR. 34.

IF you seek truth you will not seek to conquer by all possible means ; and when you have found truth, you will have a security against being conquered.

E. FR. 35.

TRUTH conquers by itself, opinions by foreign aids.

E. FR. 36.

THE soul resembles a vessel filled with water : the appearances of things resemble a ray falling upon its surface. If the water is moved, the ray will seem to be moved likewise, though it is in reality without motion. Whenever. therefore, anyone is seized with a swimming in his head, it is not the arts and virtues that are confounded, but the mind in which they are ; and, if this recover its composure, so will they likewise.

E. D. iii. 3, 6.

IF anybody shall reprove me, and shall make it apparent unto me, that in any either opinion or action of mine I do err, I will most gladly retract. For it is the truth that I seek after, by which I am sure that never any man was hurt; and as sure, that he is hurt that continueth in any error, or ignorance whatsoever

M. A. vi 60.

TEACH them that sin better, and make it appear unto them : but be not angry with them.

M. A. vi. 25.

WHEN thou hast done well, and another is benefited by thy action, must thou like a very fool look for a third thing besides, as that it may appear unto others also that thou hast done well, or that thou mayest in time, receive one good turn for another ?

M. A vii 43.

SUCH there be, who when they have done a good turn to any, are ready to set them on the score for it, and to require retaliation. Others there be, who though they stand not upon retaliation, to require any, yet they think with themselves nevertheless, that such a one is their debtor, and they know (as their word is) what they have done. Others again there be, who when they have done any such thing, do not so much as know what they have done ; but are like unto the vine, which beareth her grapes, and when once she hath borne her own proper fruit, is contented and seeks for no further recompense. As a horse after a race, and a hunting dog when he hath hunted, and a bee when she hath made her honey, look not for applause and commendation ; so neither doth that man that rightly doth understand his own nature when he hath done a good turn : but from one oth proceed to do another, even as the vine after she hath once borne fruit in her own proper season, is ready for another time. Thou therefore must be one of them, who what they do, barely do it without any further thought, and are in a manner insensible of what they do.

M. A. 5, 6

IF anyone opposes very evident truths, it is not easy to find a reason which may persuade him to alter his opinion. This arises neither from his own strength, nor from the weakness of his teacher: but when, after being driven upon an absurdity, he becomes petrified, how shall we deal with him any longer by reason?

Now there are two sorts of petrifaction: the one, a petrifaction of the understanding; the other, of the sense of shame, when a person hath obstinately set himself not to assent to evident truths, nor to quit the defence of contradictions We all dread a bodily mortification; and would make use of every contrivance to avoid it: but none of us is troubled about a mortification of the soul. And yet, indeed, even with regard to the soul, when a person is so affected as not to apprehend or understand anything, we think him in a sad condition. but where the sense of shame and modesty is under an absolute mortification, we go so far as even to call this, strength of mind.

E. D. i. 5, 1, 2.

DELIBERATE much before you say and do anything; for, it will not be in your power to recall what is said or done.

E. FR. 96.

REMEMBER, that to change thy mind upon occasion, and to follow him that is able to rectify thee, is equally ingenuous, as to find out at the first, what is right and just, without help. For of thee nothing is required, that is beyond the extent of thine own deliberation and judgment, and of thine own understanding.

M. A. viii. 14.

SOLON, when he was silent at an entertainment, being asked by Periander whether he was silent for want of words, or from folly: "No fool," answered he, "can be silent at a feast."

E. FR. 71.

I F you would give a just sentence, mind neither parties nor pleaders, but the cause itself.

E. FR. 56.

THESE two rules, thou must have always in a readiness. First do nothing at all, but what Reason proceeding from the regal and supreme part, shall for the good and benefit of men, suggest unto thee. And secondly, if any man that is present, shall be able to rectify thee or to turn thee from some erroneous persuasion, that thou be always ready to change thy mind, and this change to proceed, not from any respect of any pleasure or credit thereon depending, but always from some probable apparent ground of justice, or of some public good thereby to be furthered ; or from some other such inducement.

M. A. IV. 10

SUCH is the present case.   Because by speech and verbal precepts we are to arrive at perfection, and purify our own choice, and rectify that faculty, of which the office is, the use of the appearances of things ; and because for the delivery of theorems a certain manner of expression, and some variety and subtlety of discourse, becomes necessary ; many, captivated by these very things —one by expression, another by syllogisms, a third by convertible propositions, just as our traveller was by the good inn—go no further, but sit down and waste their lives shamefully there, as if amongst the sirens.   Your business, man, was to prepare yourself for such an use of the appearances of things as nature demands : not to be frustrated of your desires, or incur your aversions ; never to be disappointed or unfortunate, but free, unrestrained, uncompelled ; conformed to the administration of Jupiter, obedient to that, finding fault with nothing, but able to say from your whole soul the verses which begin,

Conduct me, Jove ; and thou, O Destiny.

E. D. ii. 23, 4.

234

Un   · ®

H E who frequently converses with others, either in discourse or entertainments, or in any familiar way of living, must necessarily either become like his companions, or bring them over to his own way. For, if a dead coal be applied to a live one, either the first will quench the last, or the last kindle the first. Since, then, the danger is so great, caution must be used in entering into these familiarities with the vulgar; remembering that it is impossible to touch a chimney-sweeper without being partaker of his soot.

E. D iii. 16, 1.

I T is not thine, but another man's sin. Why should it trouble thee? Let him look to it, whose sin it is.

M. A. ix. 18.

C HOOSE the best life; for custom will make it pleasant

Attributed to EPICTETUS.

Un   ®

THE form of the Athenians' prayer did run thus; "O rain, rain good Jupiter, upon all the grounds and fields that belong to the Athenians." Either we should not pray at all, or thus absolutely and freely; and not everyone for himself in particular alone.

M. A. v. 7.

A MAN should come to sacrifices and prayers, previously purified. But you, when you have got the words by heart, say, "These words are sacred of themselves."

E. D. iii. 21, 1.

TAKE me and throw me where thou wilt: I am indifferent. For there also I shall have that Spirit which is within me propitious; that is well pleased and fully contented both in that constant disposition, and with those particular actions, which to its own proper constitution are suitable and agreeable.

M. A. viii. 43.

236

HEALTH is a good, sickness an evil. No, sir. But what? A right use of health is good, a wrong one evil. So that in truth it is possible to be a gainer even by sickness.

E. D. iii. 20, 1.

AS one who had lived, and were now to die by right, whatsoever is yet remaining, bestow that wholly as a gracious overplus upon a virtuous life. Love and affect that only, whatsoever it be that happeneth, and is by the Fates appointed unto thee. For what can be more reasonable? And as anything doth happen unto thee by way of cross, or calamity, call to mind presently and set before thine eyes, the examples of some other men, to whom the selfsame thing did once happen likewise. Well, what did they? They grieved; they wondered; they complained. And where are they now?

M. A. vii. 31.

YOU will commit the fewest faults in judging, if you are faultless in your own life.

E. FR. 57.

USE thyself, as often as thou seest any man do anything, presently if it be possible to say unto thyself, What is this man's end in this his action? But begin this course with thyself first of all, and diligently examine thyself concerning whatsoever thou doest.

·M. A. x. 37.

PIERCE and penetrate into the estate of every-one's understanding that thou hast to do with: as also make the estate of thine own open, and penetrable to any other.

M. A. viii. 58.

A LIFE entangled with fortune resembles a wintry torrent; for it is turbulent, and muddy, and difficult to pass, and violent, and noisy, and of shorter continuance.

A soul conversant with virtue resembles a perpetual fountain; for it is clear, and gentle, and potable, and sweet, and communicative, and rich, and harmless, and innocent.

E. FR. 1.

THOU must be like a promontory of the sea, against which though the waves bear continually, yet it both itself stands, and about it are those swelling waves stilled and quieted.

M. A. iv. 40.

UNSPOTTED by pleasure, undaunted by pain; free from any manner of wrong, or contumely, by himself offered unto himself: not capable of any evil from others: a wrestler of the best sort, and for the highest prize.

M. A. iii. 4.

239

Un   ®

THE will of nature may be learned from those things in which we do not differ from each other. As, when our neighbour's boy hath broken a cup, or the like, we are presently ready to say, "These are things that will happen." Be assured, then, that when your own cup likewise is broken, you ought to be affected just as when another's cup was broken. Transfer this, in like manner, to greater things. Is the child or wife of another dead? There is no one who would not say, "This is an accident common to man." But if anyone's own child happens to die, it is presently, "Alas! how wretched am I!" But it should be remembered how we are affected in hearing the same thing concerning others

E. M. 26.

I, TOO, the other day had an iron lamp burning before my household deities. Hearing a noise at the window, I ran. I found my lamp was stolen. I considered, that he who took it away did nothing unaccountable. What then? To-morrow, says I, you shall find an earthen one; for a man loses only what he hath. I have lost my coat. Ay, because you had a coat. I have a pain in my head. Why, can you have a pain in your horns? Why, then, are you out of humour? For loss and pain can be only of such things as are possessed.

E. D. i. 18, 1.

THOU seest that those things, which for a man to hold on in a prosperous course, and to live a divine life, are requisite and necessary, are not many, for the gods will require no more of any man, that shall but keep and observe these things.

M. A. ii. 2.

APPEARANCES to the mind are of four kinds. Things either are what they appear to be; or they neither are, nor appear to be; or they are, and do not appear to be; or they are not, and yet appear to be. To form a right judgment in all these cases, belongs only to the completely instructed.

E. D. i. 27, 1.

AGAINST specious appearances we must have clear preconceptions brightened up and ready. When death appears as an evil, we ought immediately to remember that evils may be avoided, but death is necessity.

Ibid.

WHAT is the cause of assent to anything? Its appearing to be true. It is not possible then, to assent to what appears to be not true. Why? Because it is the very nature of the understanding to agree to truth, to be dissatisfied with falsehood, and to suspend its belief in doubtful cases. What is the proof of this? Persuade yourself if you can, that it is now night. Impossible. Unpersuade yourself that it is day. Impossible. When anyone then assents to what is false, be assured that he doth not wilfully assent to it as false; but what is false appears to him to be true.

E D. i. 28, 1.

WILL you say that there is nothing independent which is in your own power alone,
and unalienable? See, then, if you have anything of this sort.—"I do not know" But, consider it thus: Can anyone make you assent to a
falsehood?—"No one." In the topic of assent,
then, you are unrestrained and unhindered.—
"Agreed." Well, and can anyone compel you to
exert your pursuits towards what you do not like?
—"He can. For when he threatens me with
death, or fetters, he compels me to exert them."
If, then, you were to despise dying, or being
fettered, would you any longer regard him?—
"No." Is despising death, then, an action in
our power, or is it not?—"It is." Is it, therefore,
in your power also to exert your pursuits towards
anything, or is it not?—"Agreed that it is. But
in whose power is my avoiding anything?" This
too, is in your own.—"What then, if, when I am
exerting myself to walk, anyone should restrain
me?" What part of you can he restrain? Can
he restrain your assent?—"No, but my body."
Ay, as he may a stone.—"Be it so. But still I
walk no more." And who told you that walking
was an action of your own that cannot be restrained? For I only said that your exerting yourself towards it could not be restrained.

E. D. iv. 1, 11.

Un   · ®

B^Y placing over against you the imitation of
great and good men, you will conquer any
appearance, and not be drawn away by it. But,
in the first place, be not hurried along with it, by
its hasty vehemence : but say, Appearance, wait
for me a little. Let me see what you are, and
what you represent. Let me try you. Then, afterwards, do not suffer it to go on drawing gay
pictures of what will follow : if you do, it will lead
you wherever it pleases. But rather oppose to it
some good and noble appearance, and banish this
base and sordid one. If you are habituated to
this kind of exercise, you will see what shoulders,
what nerves, what sinews, you will have. But now
it is mere trifling talk, and nothing more. He is
the true practitioner who exercises himself against
such appearances as these.

E. D. ii. 18, 5.

SEPTEMBER I

STAY, wretch, do not be hurried away. The combat is great, the achievement divine; for empire, for freedom, for prosperity, for tranquillity. Remember God. Invoke Him for your aid and protector, as sailors do Castor and Pollux in a storm. For what storm is greater than that which arises from violent appearances, contending to overset our reason? Indeed, what is the storm itself, but appearance? For, do but take away the fear of death, and let there be as many thunders and lightnings as you please, you will find that, in the ruling faculty, all is serenity and calm. but if you are once defeated, and say you will get the victory another time, and then the same thing over again; assure yourself, you will at last be reduced to so weak and wretched a condition, that you will not so much as know when you do amiss; but you will even begin to make defences for your behaviour, and thus verify the saying of Hesiod: "With constant ills the dilatory strive."

E. D ii. 18, 5.

WHETHER we ought to believe, or to disbelieve, what is said; or whether, if we do believe, we ought to be moved by it or not, what is it that tells us? Is it not the faculty of choice? Again, the very faculty of elocution, and that which ornaments discourse, if there be any such peculiar faculty, what doth it more than merely ornament and arrange expressions, as curlers do the hair? But whether it be better to speak or to be silent; or better to speak in this or in that manner; whether this be decent or indecent, and the season and use of each; what is it that tells us, but the faculty of choice?

E. D. ii. 23, 1.

Un   ®

WHAT then, would you have it appear and bear testimony against itself? What means this? If the case be thus, that which serves may be superior to that to which it is subservient; the horse to the rider; the dog to the hunter; the instrument to the musician; or servants to the king. What is it that makes use of all the rest? Choice. What takes care of all? Choice. What destroys the whole man, at one time by hunger; at another by a rope or a precipice? Choice. Hath man, then, anything stronger than this? And how is it possible, that what is liable to restraint should be stronger than what is not? What hath a natural power of hindering the faculty of sight? Both choice, and what depends on choice. And it is the same of the faculties of hearing and speech. And what hath a natural power of hindering choice? Nothing independent on itself, only its own perversion. Therefore choice alone is vice, choice alone is virtue.

E. D ii. 23, 1.

I F these things are true, and we are not stupid or acting a part when we say that the good or ill of man consists in choice, and that all besides is nothing to us, why are we still troubled? Why do we still fear? What hath been our concern is in no one's power; what is in the power of others we do not regard. What embarrassment have we left?

But direct me.

Why should I direct you? Hath not God directed you? Hath He not given you what is your own, incapable of restraint or hindrance; and what is not your own, liable to both? What directions, then, what orders have you brought from Him? "By all methods keep what is your own: what belongs to others do not covet. Honesty is your own; a sense of virtuous shame is your own. Who, then, can deprive you of these? Who can restrain you from making use of them but yourself? And how do you do it? When you make that your concern which is not your own, you lose what is." Having such precepts and directions from God, what sort do you still want from me? Am I better than He? More worthy of credit? If you observe these, what others do you need? Or are not these directions His?

E. D. i 25, 1

THE first difference between one of the vulgar and a philosopher is this : the one says, I am undone on the account of my child, my brother, my father ; but the other, if ever he be obliged to say, I am undone ¹ reflects, and adds, On account of myself. For choice cannot be restrained or hurt by anything to which choice doth not extend, but only by itself. If, therefore, we always would incline this way, and, whenever we are unsuccessful, would lay the fault on ourselves, and remember that there is no cause of perturbation and inconstancy but principle, I engage we should make some proficiency. But we set out in a very different way, from the very beginning. In infancy, for example, if we happen to stumble, our nurse doth not chide us, but beats the stone. Why, what harm hath the stone done ? Was it to move out of its place for the folly of your child ? Again, if we do not find something to eat when we come out of the bath, our governor doth not try to moderate our appetite, but beats the cook.

E. D. iii. 19.

.

FROM this day forward, whenever we do anything wrong we will impute it only to the
principle from which we act; and we will endeavour to remove that, and cut it up by the
roots with greater care than we would wens and
tumours from the body. In like manner, we will
ascribe what we do right to the same cause; and
we will accuse neither servant, nor neighbour, nor
wife, nor children as the causes of any evils to
us; persuaded that if we had not such principles,
such consequences would not follow. Of these
principles we ourselves, and not externals, are
the masters.

E. D. 1. 11, 3.

THOROUGHLY consider, how man's life is
but for a very moment of time, and so depart
meek, and contented: even as if a ripe Olive
falling, should praise the ground that bare her,
and give thanks to the tree that begat her.

M. A. iv. 39.

IS that shameful to you which is not your own act? Of which you are not the cause? Which hath happened to you by accident, like a fever, or the headache? If your parents were poor, or left others their heirs, or, though they are living, do not assist you, are these things shameful for you? Is this what you have learned from the philosophers? Have you never heard, that what is shameful is blamable; and what is blamable deserves to be blamed? Whom do you blame for an action not his own, which he hath not done himself?

E. D. iii. 26, 1.

SHAME doth not consist in not having anything to eat, but in not having reason enough to exempt you from fear and sorrow.

E. D. iii. 24, 7.

REQUIRE not things to happen as you wish, but wish them to happen as they do happen, and you will go on well.

E. M. 8.

FIT and accommodate thyself to that estate and to those occurrences, which by the destinies have been annexed unto thee; and love those men whom thy fate it is to live with; but love them truly. An instrument, a tool, an utensil, whatsoever it be, if it be fit for the purpose it was made for, it is as it should be, though he perchance that made and fitted it, be out of sight and gone. But in things natural, that power which hath framed and fitted them, is and abideth within them still : for which reason she ought also the more to be respected, and we are the more obliged (if we may live and pass our time according to her purpose and intention) to think that all is well with us, and according to our own minds. After this manner also, and in this respect, it is that he that is all in all doth enjoy his happiness.

M. A. vi. 35.

A GOOD eye must be good to see whatsoever is to be seen, and not green things only. For that is proper to sore eyes. So must a good ear, and a good smell be ready for whatsoever is either to be heard, or smelt: and a good stomach as indifferent to all kinds of food, as a millstone is, to whatsoever she was made for, to grind. As ready therefore must a sound understanding be for whatsoever shall happen. But he that saith, O that my Children might live! and, O that all men might commend me for whatsoever I do! is an eye that seeks after green things; or as teeth, after that which is tender.

M. A. A. 25.

"WHAT, then, must my leg be lame?" And is it for one paltry leg, wretch, that you accuse the world? Why will you not give it up to the whole? Why will you not withdraw yourself from it? Why will you not gladly yield it to him who gave it? And will you be angry and discontented with the decrees of Jupiter, which he, with the Fates who spun in his presence the thread of your birth, ordained and appointed? Do not you know how very small a part you are of the whole? That is, as to body; for as to reason you are neither worse, nor less, than the gods. For reason is not measured by length or height, but by principles. Will you not therefore place your good there, where you are equal to the gods?

E. D. i. 12, 3.

WHEN a person maintains his proper station
in life, he doth not gape after externals.
What would you have, man?

"I am contented if my desires and aversions
are conformable to nature: if I manage my powers
of pursuit and avoidance, my purposes and intentions and assent, in the manner I was formed
to do."

Why, then, do you walk as if you had swallowed
a spit?

"I could wish, moreover, to have all who meet
me admire me, and all who follow me cry out,
What a great philosopher!"

Who are those by whom you would be admired?
Are they not the very people who you used to say
were mad? What, then, would you be admired
by madmen?

E. D. i. 21.

A S long as the foot doeth that which belongeth unto it to do, and the hand that which belongs unto it, their labour, whatsoever it be, is not un- natural. So a man as long as he doeth that which is proper unto a man, his labour cannot be against nature ; and if it be not against nature, then neither is it hurtful unto him. But if it were so that happiness did consist in pleasure : how came notorious robbers, impure abominable livers, parricides, and tyrants, in so large a measure to have their part of pleasures ?

M. A. vi. 31.

D OTH either the Sun take upon him to do that which belongs to the rain ? or his son Æsculapius that, which unto the Earth doth properly belong ? How is it with every one of the stars in particular ? Though they all differ one from another, and have their several charges and functions by themselves, do they not all nevertheless concur and co-operate to one end ?

M. A. vi. 38.

WHAT shall I do, then?
What do you do when you come out of a
ship? Do you take away the rudder or the oars
along with you? What do you take, then? Your
own: your bottle, and your bundle. So in the
present case, if you will remember what is your
own, you will not claim what belongs to others.
Are you bid to put off your consular robe? Well,
I am in my equestrian.—Put off that too. Well,
I am naked.—Still, you raise my envy. Then
e'en take my whole body. If I can throw off a
paltry body, am I any longer afraid of a tyrant?

E. D. i. 24, 2.

Un   ®

" IS not my hand my own?" It is a part of
you, but it is by nature clay, liable to restraint, to compulsion, a slave to everything
stronger than itself.   And why do I say your
hand?   You ought to possess your whole body
as a paltry ass with a pack-saddle on, as long as
may be, as long as it is allowed you.   But if there
should come a press and a soldier should lay hold
on it, let it go.   Do not resist or murmur, otherwise you will be first beat, and lose the ass after
all.   And, since you are to consider the body
itself in this manner, think what remains to do
concerning those things which are provided for the
sake of the body.   If that be an ass, the rest are
bridles, pack-saddles, shoes, oats, hay, for the ass.
Let these go too.   Quit them more easily and
expeditiously than the ass.

E. D iv. 1, 12.

AND when you are thus prepared and thus exercised to distinguish what belongs to others from your own; what is liable to restraint from what is not; to esteem your own property, the other not; to keep your desire, to keep your aversion carefully turned to this point; whom have you any longer to fear?—"No one." For about what should you be afraid? About what is your own, in which consists the essence of good and evil? And who hath any power over this? Who can take it away? Who can hinder you? No more than God can be hindered. But are you afraid for body, for possessions, for what belongs to others, for what is nothing to you? And what have you been studying all this while, but to distinguish between your own and not your own, what is in your power and what is not in your power; what is liable to restraint and what is not?

E. D. iv. 1, 12.

Un   ⓡ

HE hath a stronger body, and is a better wrestler than I. What then? Is he more bountiful? is he more modest? Doth he bear all adverse chances with more equanimity: Or with his neighbour's offences with more meekness and gentleness than I?

M. A. vii. 28.

A VERY ridiculous thing it is, that any man should dispense with vice and wickedness in himself, which is in his power to restrain; and should go about to suppress it in others, which is altogether impossible.

M. A. vii. 41.

UPON every accident, remember to turn towards yourself and inquire what powers you have for making a proper use of it. If you see a handsome person, you will find continence a power against this · if pain be presented to you, you will find fortitude : if ill language, you will find patience. And thus habituated, the appearances of things will not hurry you away along with them.

E. M. 10.

BE not elated on any excellence not your own. If a horse should be elated and say, " I am handsome," it would be supportable. But when you are elated, and say, " I have a handsome horse," know that you are elated on what is, in fact, only the good of the horse.

E. M. 6.

H E is a man of sense who doth not grieve for what he hath not, but rejoices in what he hath.

E. FR. 124.

H E that hath broken off the bonds of the body, and perceiving that in a very little while he must of necessity bid the World farewell, and leave all these things behind him, he wholly applied himself, as to righteousness in all his actions, so to the common Nature in all things that should happen unto him And contenting himself with these two things, to do all things justly, and whatsoever God doth send to like well of it : what others shall either say or think of him, or shall do against him, he doth not so much as trouble his thoughts with it. To go on straight, whither right and reason directed him, and by so doing to follow God, was the only thing that he did mind, that, his only business and occupation.

M. A. x. 10.

THE more rarely the objects of pleasure occur, the more delightful they are.

E. FR. 49.

LET not that chief commanding part of thy soul be ever subject to any variation through any corporal either pain or pleasure, neither suffer it to be mixed with these, but let it both circumscribe itself, and confine those affections to their own proper parts and members. But if at any time they do reflect, and rebound upon the mind and understanding (as in an united and compacted body it must needs;) then must thou not go about to resist sense and feeling, it being natural. However let not thy understanding to this natural sense and feeling, which whether unto our flesh pleasant or painful, is unto us nothing properly, add an opinion of either good or bad, and all is well.

M. A. v. 20.

PASSION is produced no otherwise than by a disappointment of the desires, and an incurring of the aversions. It is this which introduces perturbations, tumults, misfortunes, and calamities; this is the spring of sorrow, lamentation, and envy; this renders us envious, and emulous, and incapable of hearing reason.

E. D. iii. 2, 2.

THIS faculty in particular we have received from nature, that whatsoever doth oppose itself unto her, and doth withstand her in her purposes and intentions, she doth, though against its will and intention, bring it about to herself, to serve herself of it in the execution of her own destined ends; and so by this though not intended co-operation of it with herself makes it part of herself whether it will or no. So may every reasonable Creature, what crosses or impediments soever it meets with in the course of this mortal life, it may use them as fit and proper objects, to the furtherance of whatsoever it intended, and absolutely proposed unto itself as its natural end and happiness.

M. A. viii. 33.

" FOR what purpose have I received these things ? "—To use them. " How long ? "— As long as he who lent them pleases. If, then, they are not necessary, do not attach yourself to them, and they will not be so ; do not tell yourself that they are necessary, and they are not.

This should be our study from morning till night, beginning from the least and frailest things, from an earthen vessel, from a glass. Afterwards, proceed to a suit of clothes, a dog, a horse, an estate ; from thence to yourself, body, parts of the body, children, wife, brothers. Look everywhere around you, and throw them from yourself. Correct your principles. See that nothing cleave to you which is not your own ; nothing grow to you that may give you pain when it is torn away. And say, when you are daily exercising yourself as you do here, not that you act the philosopher (admit this to be an insolent title), but that you are asserting your freedom. For this is true freedom. This is the freedom that Diogenes gained from Antisthenes, and declared it was impossible that he should ever after be a slave to anyone.

E. D. iv. 1, 13.

265

WHAT room is there, then, for quarrelling to a person thus disposed? For doth he wonder at anything that happens? Doth it appear new to him? Doth not he expect worse and more grievous injuries from bad people than happen to him? Doth he not reckon it so much gained, as they come short of the last extremities? Such a one hath reviled you.—You are much obliged to him that he hath not struck you.— But he hath struck you too. — You are much obliged to him that he hath not wounded you too —But he hath wounded you too.—You are much obliged to him that he hath not killed you. For when did he ever learn, or from whom, that he is a gentle, that he is a social animal, that the very injury itself is a great mischief to the injurious? As, then, he hath not learned these things, nor believes them, why should he not follow what appears for his interest? Your neighbour hath thrown stones. What then? Is it any fault of yours? But your goods are broken. What then? Are you a piece of furniture? No, but your essence consists in the faculty of choice.

E. D. iii. 5, 2.

WHAT behaviour, then, is assigned you in return? If you consider yourself as a wolf —to bite again, to throw more stones. But if you ask the question as a man, examine your treasure, see what faculties you have brought into the world with you. Are they dispositions to ferocity? to revenge? When is a horse miserable? When he is deprived of his natural faculties. Not when he cannot crow, but when he cannot run. And a dog? not when he cannot fly, but when he cannot hunt. Is not a man, then, also unhappy in the same manner? Not he who cannot strangle lions, (for he hath received no faculties for this purpose from nature) but who hath lost his rectitude of mind, and fidelity. Such a one is the person who ought to be publicly lamented for the misfortunes into which he is fallen.

E. D. iii. 5, 2.

Un   · ®

FROM some high place as it were to look down, and to behold here flocks, and there sacrifices, without number , and all kind of navigation ; some in a rough and stormy sea, and some in a calm : the general differences, or different estates of things, some, that are now first upon being ; the several and mutual relations of those things that are together ; and some other things that are at their last. Their lives also, who were long ago, and theirs who shall be hereafter, and the present estate and life of those many nations of Barbarians that are now in the world, thou must likewise consider in thy mind. And how many there be, who never so much as heard of thy Name, how many that will soon forget it ; how many who but even now did commend thee, within a very little while perchance will speak ill of thee. So that neither fame, nor honour, nor anything else that this world doth afford, is worth the while. The sum then of all ; Whatsoever doth happen unto thee, whereof God is the cause, to accept it contentedly · whatsoever thou doest, whereof thou thyself art the cause, to do it justly : which will be, if both in thy resolution and in thy action thou have no further end, than to do good unto others, as being that, which by thy natural constitution, as a man, thou art bound unto.

M A. ix. 29

LET not things future trouble thee. For if necessity so require that they come to pass, thou shalt (whensoever that is) be provided for them with the same reason, by which whatsoever is now present, is made both tolerable and acceptable unto thee. All things are linked and knitted together, and the knot is sacred, neither is there anything in the world, that is not kind and natural in regard of any other thing, or, that hath not some kind of reference, and natural correspondence with whatsoever is in the world besides. For all things are ranked together, and by that decency of its due place and order that each particular doth observe, they all concur together to the making of one and the same orderly composition.

M A. vii. 6.

AS several members are in one body united, so are reasonable creatures, in a body divided and dispersed, all made and prepared for one common operation.

M. A. vii. 10.

THAT which is not good for the beehive, cannot be good for the bee.

M. A. vi. 49.

L ET us see your principles. For is it not evident that you consider your own choice as
nothing, but look out for something external and
independent on it? As, what such a one will say
of you, and what you shall be thought: whether
a man of letters, whether to have read Chrysippus
or Antipater; for, if Archedemus too, you have
everything you wish. Why are you still solicitous,
lest you should not show us what you are? Will
you let me tell you what you have showed us that
you are? A mean, discontented, passionate,
cowardly fellow; complaining of everything; accusing everybody; perpetually restless; good for
nothing. This you have showed us.

E. D. iii. 2, 5.

WHAT is this, that now my fancy is set upon ? of what things doth it consist ? how long can it last ? which of all the virtues, is the proper virtue for this present use ? as whether meekness, fortitude, truth, faith, sincerity, contentedness, or any of the rest ? Of everything therefore thou must use thyself to say, This immediately comes from God, This by that fatal connection and concatenation of things, or (which almost comes to one) by some coincidental casualty. And as for this, it proceeds from my neighbour, my kinsman, my fellow : through his ignorance indeed, because he knows not what is truly natural unto him : But I know it, and therefore carry myself towards him according to the natural law of fellowship ; that is kindly, and justly. As for those things that of themselves are altogether indifferent, as in my best judgment I conceive everything to deserve more or less, so I carry myself towards it.

M. A. iii. 12.

CAST away from thee opinion, and thou art safe. And what is it that hinders thee from casting of it away? When thou art grieved at anything, hast thou forgotten that all things happen according to the Nature of the Universe; and that him only it concerns, who is in fault; and moreover, that what is now done, is that which from ever hath been done in the world, and will ever be done, and is now done everywhere: how nearly all men are allied one to another by a kindred not of blood, nor of seed, but of the same mind. Thou hast also forgotten that every man's mind, partakes of the Deity, and issueth from thence; and that no man can properly call anything his own, no not his son, nor his body, nor his life; for that they all proceed from that One who is the giver of all things · that all things are but opinion; that no man lives properly, but that very instant of time which is now present. And therefore that no man whensoever he dieth can properly be said to lose any more, than an instant of time.

M. A. XII. 19.

BUT show me that he who hath the worst principles gets the advantage over him who hath the better. You never will show it, nor anything like it: for the law of nature and of God is this: Let the better be always superior to the worse.

In what?

In that wherein it is better. One body is stronger than another : many than one; and a thief than one who is not a thief. Thus I, too, lost my lamp because the thief was better at keeping awake than I. But he bought a lamp at the price of being a thief, a rogue, and a wild beast. This seemed to him a good bargain, and much good may it do him !

E. D. i. 29, 4.

Un   ®

OH, wretched I! to whom this mischance is happened! nay, happy I, to whom this thing being happened, I can continue without grief; neither wounded by that which is present, nor in fear of that which is to come. For as for this, it might have happened unto any man, but any man having such a thing befallen him, could not have continued without grief. Why then should that rather be an unhappiness, than this a happiness? But however, canst thou, O man! term that unhappiness, which is no mischance to the nature of man! Canst thou think that a mischance to the nature of man, which is not contrary to the end and will of his nature? What then hast thou learned is the will of man's nature? Doth that then which hath happened unto thee, hinder thee from being just? or magnanimous? or temperate? or wise? or circumspect? or true? or modest? or free? or from anything else of all those things in the present enjoying and possession whereof the nature of man (as then enjoying all that is proper unto her,) is fully satisfied?

M. A. iv. 41.

OCTOBER I

WHEN any alarming news is brought you, always have it at hand that no news can be brought you concerning what is in your own choice. Can anyone bring you news that your opinions or desires are ill conducted? By no means; but that somebody is dead. What is that to you, then? That somebody speaks ill of you. And what is that to you, then?

E. D. iii. 18, 1.

AS for praise and commendation, view their mind and understanding, what estate they are in; what kind of things they fly, and what things they seek after: and that as in the sea-side, whatsoever was before to be seen, is by the continual succession of new heaps of sand cast up one upon another, soon hid and covered; so in this life, all former things by those which immediately succeed.

M. A. vii. 22.

WHENEVER anyone exceeds moderation, the most delightful things may become the most undelightful.

E. FR. 50.

IF you are struck by the appearance of any promised pleasure, guard yourself against being hurried away by it ; but let the affair wait your leisure, and procure yourself some delay. Then bring to your mind both points of time : that in which you shall enjoy the pleasure, and that in which you will repent and reproach yourself after you have enjoyed it ; and set before you, in opposition to these, how you will rejoice and applaud yourself if you abstain. And even though it should appear to you a seasonable gratification, take heed that its enticing and agreeable and attractive force may not subdue you ; but set in opposition to this how much better it is to be conscious of having gained so great a victory.

E. M. 34.

MEN are disturbed, not by things, but by the principles and notions which they form concerning things. Death, for instance, is not terrible, else it would have appeared so to Socrates. But the terror consists in our notion of death that it is terrible. When therefore we are hindered, or disturbed, or grieved, let us never impute it to others, but to ourselves; that is, to our own principles. It is the action of an uninstructed person to lay the fault of his own bad condition upon others; of one entering upon instruction to lay the fault on himself; and of one perfectly instructed, neither on others nor on himself.

E. M. 5.

SOCRATES used very properly to call these things vizards : for, as masks appear shocking and formidable to children, from their inexperience, we are affected in like manner, with regard to things, for no other reason than as children are with regard to vizards. For what is a child? Ignorance. What is a child? Want of learning; for, so far as the knowledge of children extends, they are not inferior to us. What is death? A vizard. Turn it, and be convinced See, it doth not bite. This little body and spirit must be separated (as they formerly were) either now, or hereafter : why, then, are you displeased if it be now ? For if not now, if will be hereafter.

E. D. ii. 1, 3.

NEVER either praise or blame any person on account of outward actions that are common to all, but on the account of principles. These are the peculiar property of each individual, and the things which make actions good or bad.

E. D. IV. 4, 5.

IS it not a cruel thing to forbid men to affect those things, which they conceive to agree best with their own natures, and to tend most to their own proper good and behoof? But thou after a sort deniest them this liberty, as often as thou art angry with them for their sins. For surely they are led unto those sins whatsoever they be, as to their proper good and commodity. But it is not so (that wilt object perchance). Thou therefore teach them better, and make it appear unto them : but be not thou angry with them.

M. A. vi. 25.

IN a voyage, for instance, casting my eyes down upon the ocean below, and looking round me and seeing no land, I am out of my wits, and imagine that if I should be shipwrecked I must swallow all that ocean; nor doth it once enter my head, that three pints are enough to do my business. What is it then that alarms me? The ocean? No, but my own principle. Again, in an earthquake, I imagine the city is going to fall upon me; but is not one little stone enough to knock my brains out? What is it then that oppresses and puts us out of our wits? Why, what else but our principles?

E. D. ii 16, 3.

"OUR wall is secure, we have provisions for a very long time, and every other preparation." These are what render a city fortified and impregnable, but nothing but its principles render the human soul so. For what wall is so strong, what body so impenetrable, or what possession so unalienable, or what dignity so secured against stratagems? All things else, everywhere else, are mortal, easily reduced ; and whoever in any degree fixes his mind upon them, must necessarily be subject to perturbation, despair, terrors, lamentations, disappointed desires, and incurred aversions.

E. D. iv. 5, 3.

THE things or objects themselves, reach not unto the soul, but stand without still, and quiet, and that it is from the opinion only which is within, that all the tumult and all the trouble doth proceed.

M. A. iv. 3.

OUTWARD pomp and appearance, is a great juggler; and then especially art thou most in danger to be beguiled by it, when (to a man's thinking) thou most seemest to be employed about matters of moment.

M. A. 6, 4.

PUBLIC shows and solemnities with much pomp and vanity, stage plays, flocks and herds; conflicts and contentions: a bone thrown to a company of hungry curs; a bait for greedy fishes; the painfulness, and continual burden-bearing of wretched ants, the running to and fro of terrified mice: little puppets drawn up and down with wires and nerves: these be the objects of the World.

M. A. 7, 3.

THE best kind of revenge is, not to become like unto them.

M. A. 6, 5.

LET this be thy only joy, and thy only comfort, from one sociable kind action without intermission to pass unto another, God being ever in thy mind.

M. A. 6.

CHARITABLE actions, and a holy disposition, is the only fruit of this earthly life.

M. A. 6, 27.

TAKE heed lest at any time thou stand so affected, though towards unnatural lived men, as ordinary men are commonly one towards another.

M. A. 7, 36.

CONSIDER well whether magnanimity rather, and true liberty, and true simplicity, and equanimity, and holiness, whether these be not most kind and natural.

M. A. v. 9.

WHAT is the use that now at this present I make of my soul? Thus from time to time and upon all occasions thou must put this question to thyself, what is now that part of mine which they call the rational mistress part, employed about; Whose soul do I now properly possess? a child's? or a youth's? a woman's? or a tyrant's? some brute, or some wild beast's soul?

M. A. v. 11.

SUCH as thy thoughts and ordinary cogitations are, such will thy mind be in time. For the soul doth as it were receive its tincture from the fancies, and imaginations. Dye it therefore and thoroughly soak it with the assiduity of these cogitations.

M. A. v. 15.

HEREIN doth consist happiness of life, for a man to know thoroughly the true nature of everything; What is the matter, and what is the form of it : with all his heart and soul, ever to do that which is just, and to speak the truth. What then remaineth but to enjoy thy life in a course and coherence of good actions, one upon another immediately succeeding, and never interrupted, though for never so little a while?

M. A. xii. 22.

HE that is endowed with true magnanimity, who hath accustomed himself to the contemplation both of all times, and of all things in general; can this mortal life (thinkest thou) seem any great matter unto him? It is not possible; answered he. Then neither will such a one account death a grievous thing? By no means.

M. A. vii. 23.

285

Un   ®

TO live happily is an inward power of the soul, when she is affected with indifference, towards those things that are by their nature indifferent.

M. A. xi. 15

IT is in thy power absolutely to exclude all manner of conceit and opinion, as concerning this matter; and by the same means, to exclude all grief and joy from thy soul For as for the things and objects themselves, they of themselves have no such power, whereby to beget and force upon us any opinion at all.

M. A. vi. 47.

DOST thou grieve that thou dost weigh but so many pounds, and not 300 rather? Just as much reason hast thou to grieve that thou must live but so many years, and not longer. For as for bulk and substance thou dost content thyself with that proportion of it that is allotted unto thee, so shouldst thou for time.

M. A. vi. 45.

I F, then, the things independent on choice are neither good nor evil; and all that do depend on choice are in our own power, and can neither be taken away from us, nor given to us, unless we please, what room is there left for solicitude? But we are solicitous about this paltry body or estate of ours, or about the determination of Cæsar, and not at all about anything internal. Are we ever solicitous not to take up a false opinion? No, for this is in our own power. Or not to exert our pursuits contrary to nature? No, nor this neither. When, therefore, you see anyone pale with solicitude, as the physician pronounces from the complexion that such a patient is disordered in the spleen, another in the liver, so do you likewise say, this man is disordered in his desires and aversions, he cannot walk steady, he is in a fermentation. For nothing else changes the complexion or causes a trembling or sets the teeth a-chattering.

E. D. ii. 13, 2.

THUS are we too affected. What do we admire? Externals. For what do we strive? Externals. And are we, then, in any doubt how we come to fear and be solicitous? What is the consequence, then, when we esteem the things that are brought upon us to be evils? We cannot but fear; we cannot but be solicitous. And then we say, "O Lord God, how shall I avoid solicitude!" Have you not hands, fool? Hath not God made them for you? Sit down now and pray that your nose may not run! Wipe it rather, and do not murmur. Well: and hath He given you nothing in the present case? Hath not He given you patience? Hath not He given you magnanimity? Hath not He given you fortitude? When you have such hands as these, do you still seek for somebody to wipe your nose? But we neither study nor regard these things.

E. D. ii. 16, 2.

Un   ℗

THE condition and characteristic of a vulgar
person is, that he never expects either benefit
or hurt from himself, but from externals. The
condition and characteristic of a philosopher is,
that he expects all hurt and benefit from himself.
The marks of a proficient are, that he censures no
one, praises no one, blames no one, accuses no
one, says nothing concerning himself as being
anybody, or knowing anything: when he is, in
any instance, hindered or restrained, he accuses
himself; and, if he is praised, he secretly laughs
at the person who praises him, and, if he is censured, he makes no defence.

E. M. 48.

OF things, some are in our power and others not. In our power are opinion, pursuit, desire, aversion, and, in one word, whatever are our own actions. Not in our power are body, property, reputation, command, and, in one word, whatever are not our own actions.

Now, the things in our power are by nature free, unrestrained, unhindered; but those not in our power, weak, slavish, restrained, belonging to others. Remember, then, that if you suppose things by nature slavish to be free, and what belongs to others your own, you will be hindered; you will lament, you will be disturbed; you will find fault both with gods and men. But if you suppose that only to be your own which is your own, and what belongs to others such as it really is, no one will ever compel you; no one will restrain you; you will find fault with no one; you will accuse no one; you will do no one thing against your will; no one will hurt you; you will not have an enemy, for you will suffer no harm.

E. M. I.

WHEN you have lost anything external, have this always at hand, what you have got instead of it; and, if that be of more value, do not by any means say, "I am a loser"; whether it be a horse for an ass, an ox for a sheep, a good action for a piece of money, a due composedness of mind for a dull jest, or modesty for indecent discourse. By continually remembering this, you will preserve your character such as it ought to be. Otherwise consider that you are spending your time in vain; and all that you are now applying your mind to, you are going to spill and overset. And there needs but little and a small deviation from reason to destroy and overset all. A pilot doth not need the same apparatus to overset a ship as to save it; but, if he turns it a little to the wind, it is lost. even if he should not do it by design, but only for a moment be thinking of something else, it is lost. Such is the case here too. If you do but nod a little, all that you have hitherto collected is gone.

E. D. iv. 3, 1.

FOR, amidst perturbations and griefs and fears, and disappointed desires and incurred aversions, how can there be any entrance for happiness? And, where there are corrupt principles, there must all these things necessarily be.

E. D. iii. 22, 6.

EVERY particular nature hath content, when in its own proper course it speeds. A reasonable nature doth then speed, when first in matter of fancies and imaginations, it gives no consent to that which is either false or uncertain. Secondly, when in all its motions and resolutions it takes its level at the common good only, and that it desireth nothing, and flieth from nothing, but what is in its own power to compass or avoid. And lastly, when it willingly and gladly embraceth, whatsoever is dealt and appointed unto it by the common Nature.

M. A viii. 6.

KEEP yourself awake. It is no inconsiderable matter you have to guard, but modesty, fidelity, constancy, enjoyment, exemption from grief, fear, perturbation; in short, freedom. For what will you sell these? Consider what the purchase is worth —"But shall I not get such a thing instead of it?"—Consider, if you do get it, what it is that you obtain for the other. I have decency; another the office of a tribune: I have modesty; he has the prætorship

E. D. iv. 3, 1.

JUSTICE cannot be preserved, if either we settle our minds and affections upon worldly things; or be apt to be deceived, or rash, and inconstant.

M. A. xi. 9.

THE great point is to leave to each thing its own proper faculty, and then to see what the value of that faculty is, and to learn what is the principal thing, and upon every occasion, to follow that and to make it the chief object of our attention; to consider other things as trifling in comparison of this; and yet, as far as we are able, not to neglect even these. We ought, for instance, to take care of our eyes; but not as of the principal thing, but only on account of the principal; because that will no otherwise preserve its own nature, than by making a due estimation of the rest, and preferring some to others. What is the usual practice, then? That of a traveller, who, returning into his own country, and meeting on the road with a good inn, being pleased with the inn, should remain at the inn. Have you forgot your intention, man? You were not travelling to this place, but only through it. "But this a fine place." And how many other fine inns are there, and how many pleasant fields? But only to be passed through in your way. The business is, to return to your country, to relieve the anxieties of your family, to perform the duties of a citizen, to marry, have children, and go through the public offices. For you did not set out to choose the finest places, but to return to live in that where you were born, and of which you are appointed a citizen

E. D. ii. 23, 3.

FOR, without strong and constant exercise, it is not possible to preserve our desire undisappointed, and our aversion unincurred , and therefore, if we suffer it to be externally employed on things independent on choice, be assured that your desire will neither gain its object, nor your aversion avoid it.

And, because habit hath a powerful influence, and we are habituated to apply our desire and aversion to externals only, we must oppose one habit to another, and where the appearances are most slippery, there oppose exercise. I am inclinable to pleasure. I will bend myself beyond a due proportion to the other side for the sake of exercise.

E. D. iii. 12, 1, 2.

AFTERWARDS you will venture into the lists at some proper season, by way of trial, if at all, to see whether appearances get the better of you as much as they used to do. But at first, fly from what is stronger than you.

E. D. iii. 12, 2.

295

LET thy chief fort and place of defence be, a mind free from passions. A stronger place, (whereunto to make his refuge, and so to become impregnable) and better fortified than this, hath no man.

M. A. viii. 46.

AND in thy passions, take it presently to thy consideration, that to be angry, is not the part of a man, but that to be meek and gentle, as it savours of more humanity, so of more manhood. That in this, there is strength and nerves, or vigour and fortitude; whereof anger and indignation is altogether void. For the nearer everything is unto dispassionateness, the nearer it is unto power. And as grief doth proceed from weakness, so doth anger. For both, both he that is angry and that grieveth, have received a wound, and cowardly have as it were yielded themselves unto their affections.

M. A. xi. 16.

TIME delivers fools from grief; and reason, wise men

E. FR. 123.

AS a pig that cries and flings when his throat is cut, fancy to thyself everyone to be, that grieves for any worldly thing and takes on. Such a one is he also, who upon his bed alone, doth bewail the miseries of this our mortal life. And remember this, that unto reasonable creatures only it is granted that they may willingly and freely submit unto Providence: but absolutely to submit, is a necessity imposed upon all creatures equally.

M. A x. 28.

ANY person may live happily in poverty; but few in wealth and power.

E. FR. 128.

TRY also how a good man's life; (of one, who is well pleased with those things whatsoever, which among the common changes and chances of this world fall to his own lot and share; and can live well contented and fully satisfied in the justice of his own proper present action, and in the goodness of his disposition for the future.) will agree with thee. Thou hast had experience of that other kind of life. make now trial of this also   Trouble not thyself any more henceforth, reduce thyself unto perfect simplicity.

M. A. iv. 21.

EVEN as if any of the gods should tell thee, thou shall certainly die to-morrow, or next day, thou wouldst not, except thou wert extremely base, and pusillanimous, take it for a great benefit, rather to die the next day after, than to-morrow, (for alas what is the difference!) so, for the same reason, think it no great matter to die rather many years after, than the very next day.

M. A. iv. 38.

GIVE what Thou wilt, and take away what Thou wilt, saith he that is well taught and truly ·modest, to Him that gives, and takes away. And it is not out of a stout, and peremptory resolution, that he saith it, but in mere love, and humble submission.

M. A. x. 16.

NEVER say of anything, "I have lost it"; but "I have restored it." Is your child dead? It is restored. Is your wife dead? She is restored. Is your estate taken away? Well, and is not that likewise restored? "But he who took it away is a bad man." What is it to you by whose hands He, who gave it, hath demanded it back again? While He gives you to possess it, take care of it; but as of something not your own, as passengers do of an inn.

E. M. 11.

"O MORTALS, whither are you hurrying?
What are you about? Why do you
tumble up and down, wretches, like blind men?
You are going a wrong way, and have forsaken
the right You seek prosperity and happiness
in a wrong place, where it is not; nor do you
give credit to another who shows you where it
is. Why do you seek it without? It is not in
body: if you do not believe me, look upon
Myro, look upon Ofellius. It is not in wealth:
if you do not believe me, look upon Crœsus,
look upon the rich of the present age, how full
of lamentation their life is. It is not in power;
for, otherwise, they who have been twice and
thrice consuls must be happy, but they are not."

E. D. iii. 22, 3

WHEN a person is possessed of some either real or imagined superiority, unless he hath been well instructed, he will necessarily be puffed up with it. A tyrant, for instance, says: "I am supreme over all."—And what can you do for me? Can you exempt my desires from disappointment? How should you? For do you never incur your own aversions? Are your own pursuits infallible? Whence should you come by that privilege? Pray, on shipboard, do you trust to yourself, or to the pilot? In a chariot, to whom but the driver? And to whom in all other arts? Just the same. In what then, doth your power consist? — "All men pay regard to me."

So do I to my desk. I wash it and wipe it; and drive a nail for the service of my oil flask.— "What then, are these things to be valued beyond me?"—No: but they are of some use to me, and therefore I pay regard to them. Why, do not I pay regard to an ass? Do not I wash his feet? Do not I clean him? Do not you know that everyone pays regard to himself, and to you, just as he doth to an ass? For who pays regard to you as a man? Show that. Who would wish to be like you?

E. D. i. 19, 1.

Un ⋅ ®

I AM better than you, for my father hath been consul. I have been a tribune, says another, and not you   If we were horses, would you say, My father was swifter than yours?   I have abundance of oats and hay, and fine trappings? What now, if while you were saying this, I should answer, "Be it so.   Let us run a race, then"?   Is there nothing in man analogous to a race in horses, by which it may be known which is better or worse?   Is there not honour, fidelity, justice?   Show yourself the better in these, that you may be the better, as a man.   But if you tell me you can kick violently, I will tell you again that you value yourself on the property of an ass.

E. D. iii. 15, 5.

I AM a better man than you, says one, for I
have many estates, and you are pining with
hunger. I have been consul, says another, I
am a governor, a third; and I have a fine head
of hair, says a fourth. Yet one horse doth not
say to another, "I am better than you, for I
have a great deal of hay and a great deal of
oats; and I have a gold bridle and embroidered
trappings"; but, "I am swifter than you." And
every creature is better or worse, from its own
good or bad qualities Is man, then, the only
creature which hath no natural good quality?
And must we consider hair, and clothes, and
ancestors to judge of him?

E. FR. 13.

Un ⓡ

" BUT I am rich," you may say, "as well as
other people."

What, richer than Agamemnon?

"But I am handsome too."

What, handsomer than Achilles?

"But I have fine hair too."

Had not Achilles finer and brighter? Yet he
neither combed it nicely, nor curled it.

"But I am strong too."

Can you lift such a stone, then, as Hector
or Ajax?

"But I am of a noble family too."

Is your mother a goddess, or your father descended from Zeus? And what good did all
this do to Achilles, when he sat crying for a
girl?

E. D. ii. 24, 2.

—

WHEN you see another in power, set against it that you have the advantage of not wanting power. When you see another rich, see what you have instead of riches; for, if you have nothing in their stead, you are miserable. But, if you have the advantage of not needing riches, know that you have something more than he hath, and of far greater value.

E. D. iv. 9, 1.

TAKE heed, lest that whilst thou dost settle thy contentment in things present, thou grow in time so to overprize them, as that the want of them (whensoever it shall so fall out) should be a trouble and a vexation unto thee.

M. A. vii. 20.

NOVEMBER 1

WHEN the Governor of Epirus had exerted himself indecently in favour of a comedian, and was, upon that account, publicly railed at; and, when he came to hear it, was highly displeased with those who railed at him: Why, what harm, says Epictetus, have these people done? They have favoured a player, which is just what you did.

E. D. iii. 4, 1.

THESE reasonings are unconnected: "I am richer than you, therefore I am better"; "I am more eloquent than you, therefore I am better." The connection is rather this: "I am richer than you, therefore my property is greater than yours"; "I am more eloquent than you, therefore my style is better than yours." But you after all own neither property nor style.

E. M. 44.

REMEMBER that it is not only the desire of riches and power that makes us mean and subject to others, but even of quiet and leisure, and learning and travelling.

E. D. iv. 4, 1.

THOU hast no opportunity to read. What then ? Hast thou not time and opportunity to exercise thyself, not to wrong thyself; to strive against all carnal pleasures and pains, and to get the upper hand of them ; to contemn honour and vainglory ; and not only not to be angry with them, whom towards thee thou dost find insensible and unthankful, but also to have a care of them still, and their welfare ?

M. A. viii. 8.

IT is impossible but that habits and faculties must either be first produced, or strengthened and increased, by corresponding actions. Hence the philosophers derive the growth of all infirmities. When you once desire money, for example, if a degree of reasoning sufficient to produce a sense of the evil be applied, the desire ceases, and the governing faculty of the mind regains its authority : whereas, if you apply no remedy, it returns no more to its former state ; but, being again excited by a corresponding appearance, it kindles at the desire more quickly than before, and, by frequent repetitions, at last becomes callous : and by this infirmity is the love of money fixed.

E. D. ii. 13, 2

A PERSON was talking with me to-day about the priesthood of Augustus. I say to him, Let the thing alone, friend: you will be at great expense for nothing. "But my name," says he, "will be written in the annals." Will you stand by, then, and tell those who read them, "I am the person whose name is written there?" But, if you could tell everyone so now, what will you do when you are dead?—"My name will remain." —Write it upon a stone and it will remain just as well. But, pray, what remembrance will there be of you out of Nicopolis?—"But I shall wear a crown of gold."—If your heart is quite set upon a crown, take and put on one of roses, for it will make the prettier appearance.

E. D. 1. 19, 5.

WHEN I hear anyone congratulated on the favour of Cæsar, I say, What hath he got? —"A province."—Hath he, then, got such principles, too, as he ought to have?—"A public charge." —Hath he, then, got with it the knowledge how to use it too? If not, why should I be thrust about any longer to get in? Someone scatters nuts and figs. Children scramble and quarrel for them, but not men, for they think them trifles.—Provinces are distributing. Let children look to it.—Money. Let children look to it. Military command, a consulship. Let children scramble for them. Let these be shut out, be beat, kiss the hands of the giver, of his slaves. But to me they are but mere figs and nuts.—"What, then, is to be done?" If you miss them, while he is throwing them, do not trouble yourself about it; but if a fig should fall into your lap, take it and eat it, for one may pay so much regard even to a fig. But if I am to stoop and throw down one, or be thrown down by another, and flatter those who are got in, a fig is not worth this, nor any other of the things which are not really good, and which the philosophers have persuaded me not to esteem as good.

E. D. iv. 7, 4.

Un   · ®

NO one who is a lover of money, a lover of
pleasure, or a lover of glory, is likewise a
lover of mankind; but only he who is a lover of
virtue.

E. FR. 10.

THAT which doth not hurt the city, itself, cannot hurt any Citizen. This rule thou must
remember to apply and make use of upon every
conceit and apprehension of wrong. If the whole
City be not hurt by this, neither am I certainly.
And if the whole be not, why should I make it
my private grievance? Art not thou then a very
fool, who for these things, art either puffed up
with pride, or distracted with cares, or canst find
in thy heart to make such moans as for a thing
that would trouble thee for a very long time?
Consider the whole Universe, whereof thou art
but a very little part, and the whole age of the
world together, whereof but a short and very
momentary portion is allotted unto thee, and all
the Fates and Destinies together, of which how
much is it that comes to thy part and share!
Again: Another doth trespass against me. Let
him look to that He is master of his own disposition, and of his own operation.

M. A. v. 19.

RICHES are not among the number of things which are good; prodigality is of the number of those which are evil; rightness of mind, of those which are good. Now, rightness of mind invites to frugality and the acquisition of things that are good; but riches invite to prodigality, and seduce from rightness of mind. It is difficult, therefore, for a rich person to be right-minded, or a right-minded person rich

E FR. 18.

FROM the gods I received that I had good Grandfathers, and Parents, a good Sister, good masters, good domestics, loving kinsmen, almost all that I have; and that I never through haste. and rashness transgressed against any of them, notwithstanding that my disposition was such, as that such a thing (if occasion had been) might very well have been committed by me, but that it was the mercy of the gods, to prevent such a concurring of matters and occasions, as might make me to incur this blame.

M A i. 14.

A S when you see a viper, or an asp, or a scor-
pion, in an ivory or gold box, you do not love
or think it happy on account of the magnificence
of the materials in which it is enclosed, but shun
and detest it because it is of a pernicious nature,
so likewise, when you see vice lodged in the midst
of wealth and the swelling pride of fortune, be not
struck by the splendour of the materials with which
it is surrounded, but despise the base alloy of its
manners.

E. FR. 17.

I S this then a thing of that worth, that for it my
soul should suffer, and become worse than it
was? as either basely dejected, or disordinately
affected, or confounded within itself, or terrified?
What can there be, that thou shouldst so much
esteem?

M A. viii. 44.

DO you not often see little dogs caressing and playing with each other, that you would say nothing could be more friendly ; but, to learn what this friendship is, throw a bit of meat between them, and you will see. Do you too throw a bit of an estate betwixt you and your son, and you will see that he will quickly wish you underground, and you him : and then you, no doubt, on the other hand, will exclaim, What a son have I brought up! He would bury me alive! Throw in a pretty girl, and the old fellow and the young one will both fall in love with her; or let fame or danger intervene, the words of the father of Admetus will be yours :

You hold life dear ; doth not your father too?

Do you suppose that he did not love his own child when he was a little one? That he was not in agonies when he had a fever, and often wished to undergo that fever in his stead? But, after all, when the trial comes home, you see what expressions he uses. Were not Eteocles and Polynices born of the same mother and of the same father? Were they not brought up, and did they not live and eat and sleep, together? Did not they kiss and fondle each other? So that anyone who saw them would have laughed at all the paradoxes which philosophers utter about love. And yet, when a kingdom, like a bit of meat, was thrown betwixt them, see what they say, and how eagerly they wish to kill each other.

E. D. ii. 22, 1.

HENCE depends every movement both of God and man; and hence good is preferred to every obligation, however near. My connection is not with my father, but with good.— Are you so hard-hearted?—Such is my nature, and such is the coin which God hath given me. If, therefore, good is made to be anything but fair and just, away go father, and brother, and country, and everything. What! Shall I overlook my own good and give it up to you? For what? "I am your father." But not my good. "I am your brother." But not my good. But, if we place it in a right choice, good will consist in an observance of the several relations of life; and then, he who gives up some externals acquires good.

E. D. iii. 3, 2.

Un   ℞

YOUR father deprives you of your money, but he doth not hurt you. Your brother will possess as much larger a portion of land than you as he pleases; but will he possess more honour, more fidelity, more fraternal affection? Who can throw you out of this possession? Not even Jupiter, for, indeed, it is not his will; but he hath put this good into my own power, and given it me like his own, uncompelled, unrestrained, and unhindered. But when anyone hath a coin different from this, for his coin whoever shows it to him may have whatever is sold for it in return. A thievish proconsul comes into the province: what coin doth he use? Silver. Show it him, and carry off what you please. An adulterer comes: what coin doth he use? Women. Take the coin, says one, and give me this trifle. "Give it me, and it is yours." Another is fond of hunting: give him a fine nag or a puppy; and, though with sighs and groans, he will sell you for it what you will, for he is inwardly compelled by another who hath constituted this coin.

E. D. iii. 3, 2.

I HAVE often wondered, how it should come to pass, that every man loving himself best, should more regard other men's opinions concerning himself, than his own.

M. A. xii. 3.

WHAT are their minds and understanding; and what the things that they apply themselves unto; what do they love, and what do they work for? Fancy to thyself the estate of their souls openly to be seen. When they think they hurt them shrewdly, whom they speak ill of; and when they think they do them a very good turn, whom they commend and extol: O how full are they then of conceit and opinion!

M. A. ix. 32.

NOVEMBER 13

.

IF a person had delivered up your body to anyone whom he met in his way, you would
certainly be angry. And do you feel no shame
in delivering up your own mind to be disconcerted
and confronted by anyone who happens to give
you ill language?

E. M. 28.

WHAT pain soever thou art in, let this
presently come to thy mind, that it is not
a thing whereof thou needest to be ashamed,
neither is it a thing whereby thy understanding,
that hath the government of all, can be made
worse.

M. A. vii. 35.

" THE philosophers talk paradoxes."
And are there not paradoxes in other arts?
What is more paradoxical than the pricking anyone's eye to make him see? If a person was to
tell this to one ignorant of surgery, would not he
laugh at him? Where is the wonder then, if in
philosophy too, many truths appear paradoxes to
the ignorant!

E. D. i. 25, 4.

318

THINK thyself fit and worthy to speak, or to
do anything, that is according to Nature,
and let not the reproach, or report of some that
may ensue upon it, ever deter thee. If it be right
and honest to be spoken or done, undervalue not
thyself so much, as to be discouraged from it.
As for them, they have their own rational over-
ruling part, and their own proper inclination:
which thou must not stand and look about to
take notice of, but go on straight

M. A v. 3

Un   ®

WHAT says Antisthenes, then? Have you never heard? "It is kingly, O Cyrus, to do well, and to be ill spoken of." My head is well, and all around me think it aches. What is that to me? I am free from a fever; and they compassionate me as if I had one. "Poor soul, what a long while have you had this fever!" I say, too, with a dismal countenance, Ay, indeed, it is now a long time that I have been ill.—"What can be the consequence, then?" What pleases God. And at the same time I secretly laugh at them who pity me. What forbids, then, but that the same may be done in the other case? I am poor, but I have right principles concerning poverty. What is it to me, then, if people pity me for my poverty? I am not in power, and others are; but I have such opinions as I ought to have concerning power, and the want of power.

E. D. iv. 6, 3.

LET them see to it who pity me. But I am
neither hungry, nor thirsty, nor cold. But,
because they are hungry and thirsty, they suppose me to be so too. What can I do for them,
then? Am I to go about making proclamation,
and saying, Do not deceive yourselves, good
people, I am very well: I regard neither poverty,
nor want of power, nor anything else, but right
principles. These I possess unrestrained. I care
for nothing further.—But what trifling is this?
How have I right principles when I am not
contented to be what I am, but am out of my
wits how I shall appear?—But others will get
more, and be preferred to me.—Why, what is
more reasonable than that they who take pains
for anything should get most in that particular
in which they take pains? They have taken
pains for power; you, for right principles.

E. D. iv. 6, 3.

Un   ®

SUPPOSE I should prove to you that you are deficient in what is most necessary and important to happiness, and that hitherto you have taken care of everything, rather than your duty; and, to complete all, that you understand neither what God or man or good or evil means? That you are ignorant of all the rest, perhaps, you may bear to be told; but if I prove to you that you are ignorant even of yourself, how will you bear with me, and how will you have patience to stay and be convinced? Not at all. You will immediately be offended and go away. And yet what injury have I done you? unless a looking-glass injures a person not handsome, when it shows him to himself such as he is. Or unless a physician can be thought to affront his patient when he says to him, "Do you think, sir, that you ail nothing? You have a fever Eat no meat to-day, and drink water." Nobody cries out here, "What an intolerable affront!" But if you say to anyone, Your desires are in a fermentation; your aversions are low; your intentions contradictory; your pursuits not conformable to nature; your opinions rash and mistaken; he presently goes away, and complains he is affronted.

E. D. ii. 14, 3.

IF you possess many things, you still want others; so that, whether you will or not, you are poorer than I.

What, then, do I want?

What you have not: constancy, a mind conformable to nature, and a freedom from perturbation. Patron or no patron, what care I? But you do. I am richer than you. I am not anxious what Cæsar will think of me. I flatter no one on that account. This I have, instead of silver and gold plate. You have your vessels of gold; but your discourse, your principles, your assents, your pursuits. your desires, of mere earthenware When I have all these conformable to nature, why should not I bestow some study upon my reasoning too?

E. D. iii. 9, 1, 2.

Un   ·℞

I AM at leisure. My mind is under no distraction. In this freedom from distraction, what shall I do? Have I anything more becoming a man than this? You, when you have nothing to do, are restless; you go to the theatre, or perhaps to bathe. Why should not the philosopher polish his reasoning? You have fine crystal and myrrhin vases; I have acute forms of reasoning. To you, all you have appears little; to me, all I have great. Your appetite is insatiable; mine is satisfied. When children thrust their hand into a narrow jar of nuts and figs, if they fill it they cannot get it out again; then they fall a-crying. Drop a few of them and you will get out the rest. And do you too drop your desire; do not covet many things, and you will get some.

E. D. iii. 9, 1, 2.

" BUT how is it possible that a man worth nothing, naked, without house or home, squalid, unattended, who belongs to no country, can lead a prosperous life?"—See, God hath sent us one to show, in fact, that it is possible. "Take notice of me, that I am without a country, without a house, without an estate, without a servant; I lie on the ground; no wife, no children, no coat, but only earth and heaven and one sorry cloak. And what do I want? Am not I without sorrow, without fear? Am not I free? Did any of you ever see me disappointed of my desire, or incurring my aversion? Did I ever blame God or man? Did I ever accuse anyone? Hath any of you seen me look discontented? How do I treat those whom you fear, and of whom you are struck with awe? Is it not like sorry slaves? Who that sees me doth not think that he sees his own king and master?" This is the language, this the character, this the undertaking, of a Cynic.

E. D. iii. 22, 5.

WHATSOEVER thou dost hereafter aspire unto, thou mayest even now enjoy and possess, if thou dost not envy thyself thine own happiness And that will be, if thou shalt forget all that is past, and for the future, refer thyself wholly to the divine providence, and shalt bend and apply all thy present thoughts and intentions, to holiness and righteousness. To holiness, in accepting willingly whatsoever is sent by the divine providence, as being that which the nature of the Universe hath appointed unto thee, which also hath appointed thee for that, whatsoever it be. To righteousness, in speaking the Truth freely, and without ambiguity; and in doing all things justly and discreetly. Now in this good course, let not other men's either wickedness, or opinion, or voice hinder thee : no, nor the sense of this thy pampered mass of flesh : for let that which suffers, look to itself.

M. A. xii. 1.

IT vexes me, say you, to be pitied. Is this your
affair, then, or theirs who pity you? And
further: How is it in your power to prevent it?—
"It is, if I show them that I do not need pity."
But are you now in such a condition as not to
need pity, or are you not?—"I think I am. But
these people do not pity me for what, if anything,
would deserve pity—my faults; but for poverty
and want of power, and sicknesses, and deaths,
and other things of that kind." Are you, then,
prepared to convince the world that none of these
things is in reality an evil; but that it is possible
for a person to be happy, even when he is poor
and without honours and power? Or are you
prepared to appear to them rich and powerful?
The last of these is the part of an arrogant, silly,
worthless fellow.

E. D. IV. 6, I.

I T is a thing very possible, that a man should be a very divine man, and yet be altogether unknown. This thou must ever be mindful of, as of this also, that a man's true happiness doth consist in very few things. And that although thou dost despair, that thou shalt ever be a good either Logician, or Naturalist, yet thou art never the further off by it from being either liberal, or modest, or charitable, or obedient unto God.

M. A. vii. 38.

W ILL any contemn me? let him look to that, upon what grounds he does it: my care shall be that I may never be found either doing, or speaking anything that doth truly deserve contempt. Will any hate me? let him look to that. I for my part will be kind and loving unto all.

M. A. xi. 12.

RUFUS used to say, If you are at leisure to praise me, I speak to no purpose. And indeed he used to speak in such a manner that each of us who heard him supposed that some person had accused us to him; he so hit upon what was done by us, and placed the faults of everyone before his eyes.

E. D. iii 23, 1.

DOTH a philosopher apply to people to hear him? Doth he not attract those who are fitted to receive benefit from him, in the same manner as the sun or their necessary food doth? What physician applies to anybody to be cured by him?

Ibid.

IT is more necessary for the soul to be cured than the body; for it is better to die than to live ill.

E FR 87.

WHEN we see anyone handle an axe awkwardly, we do not say, "Where is the use of this art? See how ill carpenters perform." But we say the very contrary, "This man is no carpenter, for he handles an axe awkwardly." So, if we hear anyone sing badly, we do not say, "Observe how musicians sing," but rather, "This fellow is no musician." It is with regard to philosophy alone that people are thus affected. When they see anyone acting contrary to the profession of a philosopher, they do not take away his title; but laying it down that he is a philosopher, and then assuming from the very fact that he behaves indecently, they infer that philosophy is of no use.

"What, then, is the reason of this?" Because we pay some regard to the preconception which we have of a carpenter and a musician and so of other artists, but not of a philosopher, which being thus vague and confused, we judge of it only from external appearances. And of what other art do we take up our judgment from the dress?

E. D. iv. 8, 1.

A S you would not wish to sail in a large and
finely decorated and gilded ship, and sink;
so neither is it eligible to inhabit a grand and
sumptuous house, and be in a storm of passions
and cares.

E. FR. 11.

A S I bear in mind that I am a part of such an
Universe, I shall not be displeased with anything that happens.   And as I have relation of
kindred to those parts that are of the same kind
and nature that I am, so I shall be careful to do
nothing that is prejudicial to the community, but
in all my deliberations shall they that are of my
kind ever be , and the common good, that, which
all my intentions and resolutions shall drive unto,
as that which is contrary unto it, I shall by all
means endeavour to prevent and avoid.   These
things once so fixed and concluded, as thou
wouldst think him an happy citizen, whose constant study and practice were for the good and
benefit of his fellow citizens, and the carriage of
the city such towards him, that he were well
pleased with it; so must it needs be with thee,
that thou shalt live a happy life.

M. A. x. 6.

YOU will confer the greatest benefits on your city, not by raising the roofs, but by exalting the souls of your fellow-citizens. For it is better that great souls should live in small habitations than that abject slaves should burrow in great houses.

E. FR. 76.

AN unmusical person is a child in music; an illiterate person, a child in learning; and an untaught one, a child in life.

E. D. iii. 19, 1.

AS it is better to lie straitened for room upon a little couch in health, than to toss upon a wide bed in sickness: so it is better to contract yourself within the compass of a small fortune and be happy, than to have a great one and be wretched.

E. F. 21.

IT is not poverty that causes sorrow, but covetous desires; nor do riches deliver from fear, but reasoning. If therefore you acquire a habit of reasoning, you will neither desire riches nor complain of poverty.

E. FR.

CHOOSE rather to punish your appetites than to be punished by them.

E. FR. 108.

WHEN you have shut your doors, and darkened your room, remember never to say that you are alone, for you are not : but God is within, and your genius is within ; and what need have they of light to see what you are doing? To this God you likewise ought to swear such an oath as the soldiers do unto Cæsar. For do they, in order to receive their pay, swear to prefer before all things the safety of Cæsar ; and will you not swear, who have received so many and so great favours, or if you have sworn, will you not stand to it ? And what must you swear? Never to disobey, nor accuse, nor murmur at any of the things appointed by him, nor unwillingly to do or suffer anything necessary. Is this oath like the former ? In the first, persons swear not to honour any other beyond Cæsar ; in the last, beyond all, to honour themselves.

E. D. i. 14, 1.

IT is better to admonish than reproach, for the one is mild and friendly, the other harsh and affronting; and the one corrects the faulty, the other only convicts them.

E. FR. 102.

ALL men are made one for another. either then teach them better, or bear with them.

M. A viii. 56.

IN general every faculty is dangerous to weak and uninstructed persons; as being apt to render them arrogant and elated. For by what method can one persuade a young man who excels in these kinds of study that he ought not to be an appendix to them, but they to him?

E. D. i. 8, 1.

CERTAINLY there is nothing better than for
a man to confine himself to necessary actions;
to such and so many only, as reason in a nature
that knows itself born for society, will command
and enjoin. This will not only procure that
cheerfulness, which from the goodness, but that
also, which from the paucity of actions doth
usually proceed. For since it is so, that most
of those things, which we either speak or do, are
unnecessary. if a man shall cut them off, it must
needs follow that he shall thereby gain much
leisure, and save much trouble, and therefore at
every action a man must privately by way of
admonition suggest unto himself, What? may not
this that now I go about, be of the number of
unnecessary actions? Neither must he use himself to cut off actions only, but thoughts and imaginations also, that are unnecessary; for so
will unnecessary consequent actions the better
be prevented and cut off.

M. A. iv. 20.

Un   ®

DECEMBER 1

NATURE has given man one tongue, but two ears, that we may hear twice as much as we speak.

Attributed to EPICTETUS.

WHETHER thou speak in the Senate, or whether thou speak to any particular person, let thy speech be always grave and modest. But thou must not openly and vulgarly observe that sound and exact form of speaking, concerning that which is truly good and truly evil, the vanity of the world and of worldly men, which otherwise truth and reason both prescribe.

M A. viii. 27.

LET not your laughter be much, nor often, nor profuse.

E. M. 33.

USE thyself when any man speaks unto thee, so to hearken unto him, as that in the interim, thou give not way to any other thoughts; that so thou mayest (as far as is possible) seem fixed and fastened to his very soul, whosoever he be that speaks unto thee.

AS we say commonly, The physician has prescribed unto this man, riding, unto another,
cold baths; unto a third, to go bare foot : so it
is alike to say, The Nature of the Universe hath
prescribed unto this man sickness, or blindness,
or some loss, or damage or some such thing.
For as there, when we say of a physician, that
he hath prescribed anything, our meaning is,
that he hath appointed this for that, as subordinate
and conducing to health.

M. A. v. 8.

THEY who have a good constitution of body
support heats and colds ; and so they who
have a right constitution of soul bear the attacks
of anger, grief, and immoderate joy, and the other
passions.

E. FR. 15.

THE time of a man's life is as a point; the substance of it ever flowing, the sense obscure; and the whole composition of the body, tending to corruption. His soul is restless, fortune uncertain, and fame doubtful: to be brief, as a stream so are all things belonging to the body; as a dream, or as a smoke, so are all that belong unto the soul. Our life is a warfare, and a mere pilgrimage. Fame after life, is no better than oblivion. What is it then that will adhere and follow? Only one thing, Philosophy. And philosophy doth consist in this, for a man to preserve that Spirit which is within him, from all manner of contumelies and injuries, and above all pains or pleasures; never to do anything either rashly, or feignedly, or hypocritically: wholly to depend from himself, and his own proper actions · all things that happen unto him to embrace contentedly, as coming from Him from whom He Himself also came; and above all things, with all meekness and a calm cheerfulness, to expect death, as being nothing else, but the resolution of those Elements, of which every creature is composed. And if the Elements themselves suffer nothing by this their perpetual conversion of one into another, that dissolution, and alteration, which is so common unto all, why should it be feared by any? Is not this according to nature? But nothing that is according to Nature, can be evil.

M. A. ii. 15.

THE soul compasseth the whole world, and
penetrateth into the Vanity, and mere out-
side (wanting substance and solidity) of it, and
stretcheth herself unto the infiniteness of eternity;
and the revolution or restoration of all things after
a certain period of time, to the same state and
place as before, she fetcheth about, and doth
comprehend in herself; and considers withal,
and sees clearly this, that neither they that shall
follow us, shall see any new thing, that we have
not seen, nor they that went before, anything
more than we: but that he that is once come
to forty (if he have any wit at all) can in a
manner (for that they are all of one kind,) see
all things, both past and future. As proper is
it and natural to the soul of man, to love her
neighbour, to be true and modest.

M. Λ. xi. 1.

Un   ⒝

WHEN children cry if their nurse happens to be absent for a little while, give them a cake, and they forget their grief. Shall we compare you to these children, then?

No, indeed. For I do not desire to be pacified by a cake, but by right principles. And what are they?

Such as a man ought to study all day long, so as not to be attached to what doth not belong to him; neither to a friend, to a place, an academy, nor even to his own body, but to remember the law and to have that constantly before his eyes. And what is the divine law? To preserve inviolate what is properly our own, not to claim what belongs to others; to use what is given us, and not desire what is not given us; and, when anything is taken away, to restore it readily, and to be thankful for the time you have been permitted the use of it, and not cry after it, like a child for its nurse and its mamma

E. D. ii. 16, 3.

FOR a man to be proud and high conceited, that he is not proud and high conceited, is of all kinds of pride and presumption the most intolerable.

M. A. xii. 20.

WHEN you have brought yourself to supply the necessities of your body at a small price, do not pique yourself upon it; nor, if you drink water, be saying upon every occasion, "I drink water." But first consider how much more sparing and patient of hardship the poor are than we. But if at any time you would inure yourself by exercise to labour, and bearing hard trials, do it for your own sake, and not for the world; do not grasp statues, but, when you are violently thirsty, take a little cold water in your mouth, and spurt it out and tell nobody.

E. M. 47.

IF you would be well spoken of, learn to speak well of others. And, when you have learned to speak well of them, endeavour likewise to do well to them; and thus you will reap the fruit of being well spoken of by them.

E. FR. 6.

O MY soul, the time I trust will be, when thou shalt be good, simple, single, more open and visible, than that body by which it is enclosed. Thou wilt one day be sensible of their happiness, whose end is love, and their affections dead to all worldly things. Thou shalt one day be full, and in want of no external thing: not seeking pleasure from anything, either living or insensible, that this World can afford; neither wanting time for the continuation of thy pleasure, nor place and opportunity, nor the favour either of the weather or of men. When thou shalt have content in thy present estate, and all things present shall add to thy content: when thou shalt persuade thyself, that thou hast all things; all for thy good, and all by the providence of the gods: and of things future also shalt be as confident, that all will do well, as tending to the maintenance and preservation in some sort, of his perfect welfare and happiness, who is perfection of life, of goodness, and beauty; Who begets all things, and containeth all things in himself, and in himself doth recollect all things from all places that are dissolved, that of them he may beget others again like unto them. Such one day shall be thy disposition, that thou shalt be able, both in regard of the gods, and in regard of men, so to fit and order thy conversation, as neither to complain of them at any time, for anything that they do; nor to do anything thyself, for which thou mayest justly be condemned.

M. A. x. i.

.

AS concerning pain: that which is intolerable is soon ended by death; and that which holds long must needs be tolerable.

M. A. vii. 22.

WHATSOEVER doth happen unto thee, thou art naturally by thy natural constitution either able, or not able, to bear. If thou beest able, be not offended, but bear it according to thy natural constitution, or as nature hath enabled thee. If thou beest not able, be not offended. For it will soon make an end of thee, and itself, (whatsoever it be) at the same time end with thee. But remember, that whatsoever by the strength of opinion, grounded upon a true apprehension of both true profit and duty, thou canst conceive tolerable: that thou art able to bear by thy natural constitution.

M. A. x. 3.

.

DO not you know that both sickness and death must overtake us? At what employment? The husbandman at his plough; the sailor on his voyage. At what employment would you be taken? For, indeed, at what employment ought you to be taken? If there is any better employment at which you can be taken, follow that. For my own part, I would be taken engaged in nothing, but in the care of my own faculty of choice, how to render it undisturbed, unrestrained, uncompelled, free. I would be found studying this, that I may be able to say to God, "Have I transgressed Thy commands? Have I perverted the powers, the senses, the preconceptions which Thou hast given me? Have I ever accused Thee, or censured Thy dispensations?"

E. D. iii. 5, 1.

" I HAVE been sick, because it was Thy pleasure ;
and so have others, but I willingly. I have
been poor, it being Thy will, but with joy. I
have not been in power, because it was not Thy
will, and power I have never desired. Hast Thou
ever seen me out of humour upon this account?
Have I not always approached thee with a cheerful
countenance, prepared to execute Thy commands
and the significations of Thy will? Is it Thy
pleasure that I should depart from this assembly?
I depart. I give Thee all thanks that Thou hast
thought me worthy to have a share in it with
Thee; to behold Thy works, and to join with Thee
in comprehending Thy administration." Let death
overtake me while I am thinking, while I am
writing, while I am reading such things as these.

E. D. iii. 5. I.

WHEREVER I go it will be well with me there, for it was well with me here, not on account of the place, but of the principles which I shall carry away with me, for no one can deprive me of these; on the contrary, they alone are my property, and cannot be taken away, and retaining them suffices me wherever I am or whatever I do   "But it is now time to die."—What is it that you call dying? Do not talk of the thing in a tragedy strain, but say, as the truth is, that it is time for a compound piece of matter to be resolved back into its original   And where is the terror of this? What part of the world is going to be lost? What is going to happen new or prodigious? Is it for this that a tyrant is formidable? Is it on this account that the swords of his guards seem so large and sharp? Try these things upon others. For my part I have examined the whole. No one hath an authority over me. God hath made me free; I know His commands; after this no one can enslave me.

E. D. iv. 7, 3.

THIS is the work, if any, that ought to employ your master and preceptor, if you had one; that you should come to him, and say: "Epictetus, we can no longer bear being tied down to this paltry body, feeding and resting and cleaning it, and hurried about with so many low cares on its account. Are not these things indifferent, and nothing to us, and death no evil? Are not we relations of God, and did we not come from Him? Suffer us to go back thither from whence we came; suffer us, at length, to be delivered from these fetters, that chain and weigh us down. Here thieves and robbers, and courts of judicature, and those who are called tyrants, seem to have some power over us, on account of the body and its possessions. Suffer us to show them, that they have no power."

And in this case it would be my part to answer: "My friends, wait for God, till He shall give the signal, and dismiss you from this service; then return to Him. For the present, be content to remain in this post where He has placed you. The time of your abode here is short, and easy to such as are disposed like you. For what tyrant, what robber, what thief, or what courts of judicature are formidable to those who thus account the body and its possessions as nothing? Stay. Depart not inconsiderately."

E. D. i. 8, 3.

LET it be thy earnest and incessant care as a Roman and a man to perform whatsoever it is that thou art about, with true and unfeigned gravity, natural affection, freedom and justice : and as for all other cares, and imaginations, how thou mayest ease thy mind of them. Which thou shalt do , if thou shalt go about every action as thy last action, free from all vanity, all passionate and wilful aberration from reason, and from all hypocrisy, and self-love, and dislike of those things, which by the fates, or appointment of God, have happened unto thee.

M. A. 2, 7.

I MUST die: and must I die groaning too?—
Be fettered. Must it be lamenting too?—
Exiled. And what hinders me, then, but that I
may go smiling, and cheerful, and serene? —
"Betray a secret."—I will not betray it; for
this is in my own power.—"Then I will fetter
you."—What do you say, man? Fetter me?
You will fetter my leg; but not Jupiter himself
can get the better of my choice. "I will throw
you into prison: I will behead that paltry body
of yours." Did I ever tell you, that I alone
had a head not liable to be cut off? — These
things ought philosophers to study; these ought
they daily to write; and in these to exercise
themselves.

E. D. i. 1, 6.

I WILL dine first, and when the hour comes,
then I will die. How? As becomes one
who restores what is not his own.

E. D. i. 1, 7.

IF I can achieve nothing myself, I will not envy another the honour of doing some gallant action. But suppose this to be a strain too high for us ; are not we capable at least of arguing thus?—Where shall I fly from death ? Show me the place; show me the people to whom I may have recourse, whom death doth not overtake. Show me the charm to avoid it. If there be none, what would you have me do? I cannot escape death; but cannot I escape the dread of it ? Must I die trembling and lamenting ? For the origin of the disease is wishing for something that is not obtained. In consequence of this, if I can bring over externals to my own inclination, I do it; if not, I want to tear out the eyes of whoever hinders me. For it is the nature of man not to bear the being deprived of good; not to bear the falling into evil. And so, at last, when I can neither bring over things to my own inclination, nor tear out the eyes of him who hinders me, I sit down and groan, and revile him whom I can; Zeus, and the rest of the gods.

E. D. i. 27, 1.

THAT soul which is ever ready, even now presently (if need be) from the body, whether by way of Extinction, or Dispersion, or Continuation in another place and estate to be separated, how blessed, and happy is it!

M. A. xi. 3

HOW many of them who came into the world at the same time when I did, are already gone out of it?

M. A. vi. 51.

OUR life is reaped like a ripe ear of corn.

M. A vii 25.

WAIT until thy soul shall fall off from that outward cloak or skin, wherein as a child in the womb it lieth involved and shut up.

M. A. ix. 3.

THUS Demetrius said to Nero: " You sentence me to death; and nature, you!" If I place my admiration on body, I give myself up for a slave; if on an estate, the same; for I immediately betray myself how I may be taken. Just as when a snake pulls in his head, I say, strike that part of him which he guards: and be you assured, that whatever you show a desire to guard, there your master will attack you. Remember but this, whom will you any longer flatter or fear?

E. D. i. 25, 3.

" BUT your head will be taken off." And will his own always remain on; or yours, who obey him ?—" But you will be thrown out un-buried." If I am the corpse, I shall be thrown out; but if I am something else than the corpse, speak more handsomely, as the thing is, and do not think to fright me. These things are frightful to children and fools.

E. D. iv. 7, 5.

Un   ®

LET that of Heraclitus never be out of thy mind, that the death of earth, is water, and the death of water, is air; and the death of air, is fire; and so on the contrary. Remember him also who was ignorant whither the way did lead, and how that Reason being the thing, by which all things in the world are administered, and which men are continually and most inwardly conversant with: yet is the thing, which ordinarily they are most in opposition with, and how those things which daily happen among them, cease not daily to be strange unto them, and that we should not either speak, or do anything as men in their sleep, by opinion and bare imagination: for then we think we speak and do, and that we must not be as children, who follow their father's example; for best reason alleging barely this: As by tradition from our forefathers we have received it.

M. A. iv. 37.

AS for death, if there be any gods, it is no grievous thing to leave the society of men. The gods will do thee no hurt thou mayest be sure. But if it be so that there be no gods, or that they take no care of the world, why should I desire to live in a world void of gods, and of all divine providence?

M. A. ii. 8

HE that feareth Death, either feareth that he shall have no sense at all, or that his senses will not be the same. Whereas, he should rather comfort himself, that either no sense at all, and so no sense of evil; or if any sense, then another life, and so no death properly.

M. A. viii. 55.

THOU must not in matter of death, carry thyself scornfully, but as one that is well pleased with it, as being one of those things that Nature hath appointed.

M. A. ix. 3.

TO look back upon things of former ages, as upon the manifold changes and conversions of several monarchies and commonwealths. We may also foresee things future, for they shall all be of the same kind ; neither is it possible that they should leave the tune, or break the consort that is now begun, as it were, by these things that are now done and brought to pass in the World. It comes all to one therefore, whether a man be a spectator of the things of this life but forty years, or whether he see them ten thousand years to-gether: for what shall he see more? "And as for those parts that came from the Earth, they shall return unto the Earth again ; and those that came from Heaven, they also shall return unto those heavenly places."

M. A. vii. 27.

THE brass pot and the earthen pitcher, as the fable says, are an unsuitable match.

E. D. iii. 12, 2.

IF you wish your children, and your wife, and your friends to live for ever, you are stupid; for you wish things to be in your power which are not so, and what belongs to others to be your own. So likewise, if you wish your servant to be without fault, you are a fool; for you wish vice not to be vice, but something else. But, if you wish to have your desires undisappointed, this is in your own power. Exercise, therefore, what is in your power. He is the master of every other person who is able to confer or remove whatever that person wishes either to have or to avoid. Whoever, then, would be free, let him wish nothing, let him decline nothing, which depends on others, else he must necessarily be a slave.

E. M. 14.

SINCE, at all events, one must die, one must necessarily be found doing something, either tilling, or digging, or trading, or serving a consulship, or sick of an indigestion or a flux. At what employment, then, would you have death find you? For my part, I would have it be some humane, beneficent, public-spirited, gallant action. But if I cannot be found doing any such great things, yet, at least, I would be doing what I am incapable of being restrained from, what is given me to do, correcting myself, improving that faculty which makes use of the appearances of things, to procure tranquillity, and render to the several relations of life their due ; and, if I am so fortunate, advancing to the third topic, a security of judging right If death overtakes me in such a situation, it is enough for me if I can stretch out my hands to God and say, " The opportunities which Thou hast given me of comprehending and following the rules of Thy administration I have not neglected. As far as in me lay, I have not dishonoured Thee. See how I have used my perceptions, how my preconceptions. Have I at any time found fault with Thee ? Have I been discontented at Thy dispensations, or wished them otherwise ? Have I transgressed the relations of life ? I thank Thee that Thou hast brought me into being. I am satisfied with the time that I have enjoyed the things which Thou hast given me. Receive them back again, and assign them to whatever place Thou wilt ; for they were all Thine, and Thou gavest them to me "

E. D. iv. 9, 2.

IT were indeed more happy and comfortable, for a man to depart out of this World, having lived all his life long clear from all falsehood, dissimulation, voluptuousness, and pride. But if this cannot be, yet is it some comfort for a man joyfully to depart as weary, and out of love with those; rather than to desire to live, and to continue long in those wicked courses. Hath not yet experience taught thee to fly from the plague? For a far greater plague is the corruption of the mind, than any certain change and distemper of the common air can be. This is a plague of creatures, as they are living creatures; but that of men as they are men or reasonable.

M. A. ix. 2.

TOYS and fooleries at home, wars abroad; sometimes terror, sometimes torpor, or stupid sloth: this is thy daily slavery.

M. A. x. 9.

CAN death be terrible to him, to whom that only seems good, which in the ordinary course of nature is seasonable? to him, to whom, whether his actions be many or few, so they be all good, is all one; and who whether he behold the things of the world being always the same either for many years, or for few years only, is altogether indifferent? O man! as a Citizen thou hast lived, and conversed in this great City the World. Whether just for so many years, or no, what is it unto thee? Thou hast lived (thou mayest be sure) as long as the Laws, and Orders of the City required; which may be the common comfort of all. Why then should it be grievous unto thee, if (not a Tyrant, nor an unjust Judge, but) the same nature that brought thee in, doth now send thee out of the world? As if the Prætor should fairly dismiss him from the stage, whom he had taken in to act a while. Oh, but the play is not yet at an end, there are but three Acts yet acted of it? Thou hast well said: for in matter of life, three Acts is the whole Play. Now to set a certain time to every man's acting, belongs unto Him only, who as first He was of thy composition, so is now the cause of thy dissolution. As for thyself, thou hast to do with neither. Go thy ways then well pleased and contented: for so is He that dismisseth thee.

M. A. xii. 27

HOW hast thou carried thyself hitherto towards the Gods ? towards thy Parents ? towards thy Brethren ? towards thy Wife ? towards thy Children ? towards thy Masters ? thy foster Fathers ? thy Friends ? thy Domestics ? thy Servants ? Is it so with thee, that hitherto thou hast neither by word nor deed wronged any of them ? Remember withal through how many things thou hast already passed, and how many thou hast been able to endure ; so that now the Legend of thy life is full, and thy charge is accomplished. Again, how many truly good things have certainly by thee been discerned? how many pleasures, how many pains hast thou passed over with contempt ? how many things externally glorious hast thou despised ? towards how many perverse unreasonable men, hast thou carried thyself kindly, and discreetly ?

M. A. v. 25.

DEATH is a cessation from the impressions of the senses, the tyranny of the passions, the errors of the mind, and the servitude of the body.

M. A. vi. 26.

IS any man so foolish as to fear change, to which all things that once were not owe their being? And what is it, that is more pleasing and more familiar to the nature of the Universe? How couldst thou thyself use thy ordinary hot baths, should not the wood that heateth them first be changed? How couldst thou receive any nourishment from those things that thou hast eaten, if they should not be changed? Can anything else almost (that is useful and profitable) be brought to pass without change? How then dost not thou perceive, that for thee also, by death, to come to change, is a thing of the very same nature, and as necessary for the nature of the Universe?

M. A. vii. 15.

Un   ℞

THE time when thou shalt have forgotten all things, is at hand. And that time also is at hand, when thou thyself shalt be forgotten by all. Whilst thou art, apply thyself to that especially which unto man as he is a man, is most proper and agreeable, and that is, for a man even to love them that transgress against him. This shall be, if at the same time that any such thing doth happen, thou call to mind, that they are thy Kinsmen; that it is through ignorance and against their wills that they sin; and that within a very short while after, both thou and he shall be no more. But above all things, that he hath not done thee any hurt; for that by him thy mind and understanding is not made worse or more vile than it was before.

M. A. vii. 16.

Un   ®

IF thou shouldst live 3000, or as many as 10,000
of years, yet remember this, that man can part
with no life properly, save with that little part of
life, which he now lives: and that which he lives,
is no other, than that which at every instant he
parts with. That then which is longest of duration,
and that which is shortest, come both to one
effect   For although in regard of that which is
already past there may be some inequality, yet
that time which is now present and in being, is
equal unto all men.   And that being it which we
part with whensoever we die, it doth manifestly
appear, that it can be but a moment of time, that
we then part with.   For as for that which is either
past or to come, a man cannot be said properly to
part with it.   For how should a man part with that
which he hath not?

E. D. ii. 12.

WHY are ears of corn produced, if it be not to ripen ? and why do they ripen, if not to be reaped ? For they are not separate individuals. If they were capable of sense, do you think they would wish never to be reaped ? It would be a curse upon ears of corn not to be reaped : and we ought to know, that it would be a curse upon man not to die ; like that of not ripening, and not being reaped. Since, then, it is necessary for us to be reaped, and we have, at the same time, understanding to know it, are we angry at it ?

E. D. ii. 6, 2.

NO great thing is brought to perfection suddenly, when not so much as a bunch of
grapes or a fig is. If you tell me that you would
at this minute have a fig, I will answer you, that
there must be time. Let it first blossom, then
bear fruit, then ripen. Is then the fruit of a fig-
tree not brought to perfection suddenly, and in
one hour : and would you possess the fruit of the
human mind in so short a time, and without
trouble ? I tell you, expect no such thing.

E. D. i. 15, 2.

WORD after word, every one by itself, must
the things that are spoken be conceived and
understood ; and so the things that are done, purpose after purpose, every one by itself likewise.

M. A. vii. 4.

WHERE, then, is the great good or evil of man?

Where his difference is. If this is preserved, and remains well fortified, and neither honour, fidelity, nor judgment is destroyed, then he himself is preserved likewise; but when any of these are lost and demolished, he himself is lost also. In this do all great events consist. Paris, they say, was undone, because the Greeks invaded Troy and laid it waste, and his family were slain in battle. By no means; for no one is undone by an action not his own. All that was only laying waste the nests of storks. But his true undoing was, when he lost the modest, the faithful, the hospitable, and the decent character. When was Achilles undone? When Patroclus died? By no means. But when he gave himself up to rage; when he wept over a girl; when he forgot that he came there not to get mistresses, but to fight. This is human undoing; this is the siege; this the overthrow: our right principles are ruined, when these are destroyed.

E. D. i. 28, 4.

THE RIVERSIDE PRESS LIMITED, EDINBURGH.

Un   ' ®

Un

Un   ˙®